"Rich in the gospel and superb in practical application, this touching book is straight up fuel for joy. Here is wisdom that should brighten your every day with sheer enjoyment of God."

MICHAEL REEVES, President and Professor of Theology, Union School of Theology

"Tim Chester's books are always unusually accessible. He can distill great amounts of complex theological truth into short, digestible chapters. In this book, he brings this skill to bear on the subject of communion with God—perhaps the greatest privilege of a Christian. But it is one little understood, and even less is it actually enjoyed. I urge you to read this book. It will make you hunger and thirst for fellowship with God."

TIMOTHY KELLER, Pastor Emeritus, Redeemer Presbyterian Church, New York City

"I absolutely loved this book. It has been a huge blessing, like cool refreshing water for my soul. I frequently found myself identifying with the sin, struggles and faulty thinking Tim Chester so vividly describes in various scenarios and illustrations, which also helped me see how my view of our triune God is often so flattened and limited. My heart was softened and warmed as Tim held up all that the Father, Son and Spirit have done, and continue to do, to enable us to truly experience and enjoy an intimate relationship with God and know his daily goodness, grace and love in the messy reality of our daily lives. I finished the book marvelling at our glorious God, feeling humbled, excited, encouraged and spurred on."

ANDREA TREVENNA, Associate Minister for Women, St Nicholas, Sevenoaks, UK; Author, *The Heart of Singleness*

"Winsome in its unpacking of theology and compelling in the sweep of its applications, *Enjoying God* is neither an essay on the Trinity nor a 'how to' manual, but something close to both. It is among the best of the rising number of books that instruct Christians on how to cross the bridge from enjoying God on the Lord's Day to enjoying God every day. Tim Chester is in no danger of making God little more than a useful utility to increase our pleasure; he is far too God-centred and gospel-centred for that. But if you desire to experience for yourself a little *more* (one of Tim's favourite words) of the truth that in God's presence there are pleasures forever more, you will be hard-pressed to find a better guide."

D.A. CARSON, Research Professor of New Testament, Trinity Evangelical Divinity School; President, The Gospel Coalition

"We talk a lot about knowing and glorifying God, but what about enjoying him? And not just as an abstract Being, but as the Father, the Son and the Holy Spirit—enjoying each Person in all of his difference as well as divine unity? And not just in happy times or at church, but in every circumstance of life? It just keeps getting better and better as you turn each page of *Enjoying God*. This book will lift you into the presence of the Source of all joy."

MICHAEL HORTON, Westminster Seminary, California

"*Enjoying God* is gourmet food for the weary soul. Tim Chester shows us how we can really, expansively, and truly enjoy our communion with God—not by any weird spiritual techniques but by drilling down into our oneness with him. As we understand the three Persons of God more richly, we are invited into a more vivid and real experience of him. This is profound truth in simple and engaging writing."

MICHAEL JENSEN, Rector, St. Mark's Darling Point, Sydney; Author, *Is Forgiveness Really Free?* and *My God, My God*

"I'm so often reassuring myself and others that feelings aren't a good sign of my spiritual state that I forget to seek and enjoy communion with God. This book reminded me of all sorts of ways in which the Lord is offering me himself to enjoy."

AGNES BROUGH, Associate Minister for Young People and Women, The Tron Church, Glasgow; Chair, Scottish Women's Bible Convention

"The best books are biblical, practical, personal, pastoral, and worshipful. *Enjoying God* is one of those rare books that excels in each area. I commend it highly."

JASON MEYER, Pastor for Preaching and Vision, Bethlehem Baptist Church

"From the authors of Scripture onwards, the Lord's people have always known that the purpose of life is 'to glorify God, and to enjoy him for ever'. But each generation, in fact every Christian, needs to discover this anew. And the way is not an easy one. But it is the only path worth taking. In *Enjoying God*, Tim Chester shares his own experiences in walking along this gospel road and issues a warm invitation to join him. Accept it, and you will never regret it."

SINCLAIR B. FERGUSON, Chancellor's Professor of Systematic Theology, Reformed Theological Seminary

TIM CHESTER

ENJOYING

GOD

Enjoying God
© Tim Chester/The Good Book Company 2018. Reprinted 2018.

Published by:
The Good Book Company

Tel (US): 866 244 2165
Tel (UK): 0333 123 0880
Email (US): info@thegoodbook.com
Email (UK): info@thegoodbook.co.uk

Websites:
North America: www.thegoodbook.com
UK: www.thegoodbook.co.uk
Australia: www.thegoodbook.com.au
New Zealand: www.thegoodbook.co.nz

ISBN: 9781784982812 | Printed in Denmark

Design by André Parker

CONTENTS

MIKE AND EMMA'S MONDAY MORNING

Sunday morning. As Mike sings he is filled with joy. His pastor has just preached on God's love to us in Christ. Mike has felt afresh that he is unworthy, but Christ is worthy. Now, as he lifts his voice in praise, his love for Christ feels strong. He has no doubt God is present in this moment. Besides, there are tears running down Emma's cheeks.

Monday morning. The day had started so well. Still buoyed by yesterday's experience at church, he'd sat down to a bacon sandwich. The kids were playing quietly in the front room. He took Emma a coffee to drink in bed and kissed her gently on the cheek. Outside the sun was shining and the birds were singing. Could life be any better?

Mike arrives at the station to find his train has been cancelled. Two train-loads of passengers are now crammed onto the next train and Mike is having to stand. He's given up any hope of reading his book. The guy pushed up against him has clearly not heard of deodorant. The next 40 minutes are not going to be fun.

Meanwhile Emma is wiping up milk from the kitchen floor. Sam and Jamie are arguing about socks. And little Poppy… Where's Poppy? Emma looks up to see the box of cornflakes topple off the kitchen table. "How can a day go so wrong so quickly?" she thinks.

Ten minutes later Emma takes a bite of toast and opens her Bible. She reads a few verses and then she closes her eyes to pray. "Father, may Mike have a good day at work. Please bless..." Jamie bursts into the room. "Where's my school sweater?" Sam's not far behind. "Have you seen my homework?" And Poppy... Where's Poppy?

Mike closes his eyes again and heads off in his imagination to a place far away from this crowded carriage. He's just about to dive into the blue water of a tropical lagoon when someone spills tea down his shirt. He swears. Immediately he flushes. And not just because warm tea is spreading across his stomach. He's embarrassed. "I'm so sorry. Really sorry. It's the delay, the standing. I'm not normally so grumpy." The young woman holding what remains of her tea is just as embarrassed. "No, no, it's my fault," she says as she squeezes past and disappears.

Back at home Emma is ushering the children out of the door. One, two, three. She thinks of Rosie. Four. Every day she thinks of Rosie, their fourth child, born with a malformed heart and dead at three months. Absent and yet always present. Two years on, Emma still feels the loss. It hurts. Here on the doorstep it hurts. "Time will heal," people had said. She knows they're trying to be positive. But she doesn't want to "be positive". Sometimes she just wants to weep.

Yesterday God had felt so present to Mike. But today... today is different. Today is over-crowded trains, sweaty passengers, a wet shirt and the all-too-present void left by little Rosie. Today God is... What is he? Not absent—Mike doesn't doubt that God is everywhere. But God doesn't exactly feel present either. Not in a way he can touch or see.

Emma's standing in the playground, chatting to other mums while Poppy pulls on her shirt. "Have you heard about Roxanne? You know, Jamal's mum? Well, I've heard…" Emma's not heard. She wants to. A bit of gossip to spice up her morning. A bit of scandal to make her feel superior. She moves in so she can hear better.

"No," she says to herself. "Don't go there. Bad idea." She turns round. Was it a bad idea? What harm would come of a little gossip? It would distract from the tedium of the day. But Emma thinks of God's word. She thinks of Christ's grace to her. She wants to show the same grace to others. "Sorry," she shouts over her shoulder, "I need to dash." Nobody notices. They're all huddled round the latest rumour.

The train is slowly coming to a halt. Mike ducks down to look out the window, hoping to see the station platform coming into view. But all he sees is a wall of graffiti. "As a result of signal failure we'll be subject to a 15-minute delay. We apologise for any inconvenience this may cause." Mike lets out an audible groan. He's not the only one. The carriage comes alive with shared grumbles.

Mike closes his eyes. He tries to recall yesterday's sermon. What had his pastor said? Something about Christ being our righteousness. Nothing new. Mike had heard it many times before. But it was such a comfort to hear again yesterday. And it is a comfort to remember it again this morning.

Meanwhile, and a little late, Emma's walking up the path to Amanda's front door. They meet most weeks to read the Bible together and pray. Emma tries to remember what it was they looked at last week. Something in Philippians. Something about knowing Christ. Whatever it was, she remembers feeling excited about it at the time.

"Sorry about the mess," says Amanda. Emma smiles. It's always messy in Amanda's house. She moves a pile of laundry off the chair onto the table so she can sit down. Amanda hands her a rather strong cup of tea. Emma doesn't know how Amanda copes with the chaos.

Half an hour late, Mike is finally sitting at his desk. "How was church?" Bob had asked. Bob is Mike's only Christian colleague. How was church? The truth is it seems a long time ago. Yesterday his pastor had spoken of a relationship with God. And on Sunday it had seemed like a real possibility. But that was Sunday and this is Monday. Today it feels so much more elusive. If only he had more time to pray, then maybe he could enjoy God. Maybe he could recreate that feeling he had enjoyed on Sunday morning. Or maybe he will just have to wait until next Sunday. Next Sunday? It is still only Monday morning.

MORE

I believe in more. More of God. More to come, to be sure, but also more now. We can know God more. *You* can know God more.

I've always enjoyed pictures and posters of the paintings of Vincent van Gogh. But seeing the paintings themselves in the Musée d'Orsay in Paris blew my mind. Their colour and movement was extraordinary. I've always enjoyed recordings of *The Lark Ascending* by Ralph Vaughan Williams. But when I heard it performed live in the Sheffield City Hall by the English Chamber Orchestra, I had to wipe the tears from my eyes. My heart was carried up on the soaring notes of the violin.

I was delighted to read recently that my football team, Sheffield United, had beaten our local rivals (a team whose name I forget). But when I was there, in the stadium, as they put goals past their opponents—that was different. Grown men hugged each other in delight. I love watching TV shows about the British countryside. But when I set off on a walk, I literally skip with joy and giggle to myself. That's not an exaggeration!

In the same way, I've always enjoyed reading about God. But to experience God himself blows my mind, brings tears to my eyes or makes me skip. And sometimes all three.

This book is about how you can experience more of God.

EXPERIENCING GOD

To help us get there, let me ask you a question. With which member of the Trinity—God the Father, God the Son or God the Spirit—do you have the strongest sense of a lived, experienced relationship? I'm not asking what you think should be the case. I'm asking you to reflect on your own experience. Why not do that now before reading on?

Over the last few years I've taken every opportunity to ask this question to lots of people in many places and among different church traditions. It's been a fascinating exercise. It's always met with a variety of responses. Some people say the Father, others the Son, others the Spirit, and others some combination. And, before you ask, there doesn't appear to be any correlation between people's answers and their church background—it's not that charismatic Christians always point to the Spirit while conservatives prefer the Father.

This book started with the realisation that for me it was the Father and the Spirit with whom I have a clear sense of a living relationship, but not the Son. I have a keen sense of the Father as the One to whom I go in prayer. I know what it is to ask him and receive from him. I don't always receive what I request, but I'm happy to trust him to organise the circumstances of my life—good and bad—for my good. And I have a strong sense of living through the Spirit's power. That's not because I'm zapping out miracles all over the place or getting tingling sensations down my spine. It's because I'm convinced that any good I do is done through the prompting and power of the Spirit. It's certainly not done in the power of Tim Chester. So I feel my dependence on the Spirit.

But I realised I had less of a sense of a present experience of the Son. I felt detached from him. I'm aware that he lived, died and rose for me so I could be reconciled to God. That's gloriously true and I'm profoundly grateful. I'm convinced all the blessings in my life flow from his work. But that was 2,000 years ago and now he's up in heaven. That's a long time ago and a long way away. What does it mean to *know* Jesus personally? And what does it mean to relate to him right now in the present?

Why does this matter?

Because I believe in more.

TWO PRINCIPLES

This book is driven by two key principles—principles that will help you enjoy God more. They're not complicated. They're not skills you need to master or achievements requiring great willpower. Yet I suspect that many Christians don't have a strong sense of relationship with God, or enjoy more of that relationship, because they don't fully appreciate these two principles. Here they are:

1. God is known through the three Persons, so we relate to the Father, the Son and the Spirit.
2. Our unity with God in Christ is the basis of our community with God in experience.

We'll come back to the second one in a moment. The first explains why relating to the three Persons of the Trinity is key to enjoying God more.

1. WE CAN KNOW GOD: THE PRINCIPLE OF THREE AND ONE

When we pray, it's all too easy to think we're praying to a thing or a force. It can seem a bit abstract. We try to imagine God, but God is invisible. How can we see the invisible God? How can finite people know the infinite? The answer is we can't! We don't have a relationship with "God" in a general sense. We can't know the essence of God—the "god-ness" of God. His nature is beyond our comprehension.

But we can know the *Persons* of God. God lives in an eternal community in which the Father, Son and Spirit relate to one another in love. And when God relates to us, he relates to us in the same way—as Father, Son and Spirit. So when we talk about having a relationship with God, that's really shorthand for having a relationship with God the Father, God the Son and God the Holy Spirit.

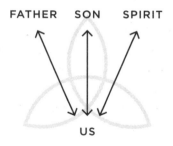

FATHER   SON   SPIRIT

US

The practical implication of this is simple: your relationship with God will be deepened and enriched if you think about how you're relating to the Father, to the Son and to the Spirit. Think how each member of the Trinity is relating to you and how you're responding to them.

When you pray, for example, think of addressing your words to the Father through the Son with the help of the Spirit. Or when you read the Bible, think of the Father revealing himself in his Son by the Holy Spirit, or think of the Son communicating his love to you through the Holy Spirit.

Stop and think about this now for a moment. How does the Father relate to you and how do you relate to him? What about the Son? And the Holy Spirit?

In this book we're going to tease out how each member of the Trinity acts towards us and how we should respond. We'll discover that the triune God—the God who is Father, Son and Spirit—is interacting with us in a thousand ways each day.

So the first step in relating to God is to relate to each distinct Person of the Trinity—Father, Son and Spirit. But we must never think of the three Persons without at the same time recognising that God is *one*. The unity of God matters because it means that to know one of the Persons is to know all three. You never relate to them on their own. This means we'll find our thoughts constantly moving from one to the other. It also means this book will be delightfully "untidy". We won't be able to talk about relating to the Father without talking about how we're loved in the Son or how the Spirit enables us to cry, "Abba, Father". We won't be able to talk about the presence of Jesus without talking about the work of the Spirit.

In the movie *The Wizard of Oz*, Dorothy and her companions set out to find the wizard of Oz, thinking he's a godlike figure who can grant them a brain, a heart and courage. Except he turns out to be a fake. There's an intimidating façade, but behind it all is a pathetic old man. The magnificent image is just a front.

People can sometimes think of God as a bit like the wizard of Oz. Jesus is the attractive face of God, but it's a façade behind which lurks a grumpy old man. Nothing could be further from the truth. The unity of the Trinity means that when we see God in Christ, we're not seeing a mask or a front. There are no surprises behind what we see in Christ. Jesus is the perfect Word of God and image of God because Jesus is God. To see the Son is to see the Father. "The Son is the radiance of God's glory and the exact representation of his being" (Hebrews 1 v 3). The Father and the Son are one being. There's not another God lurking behind the scenes. Jesus really is what God the Father is like. To relate to the Son is to relate to the Father and Spirit.

The fourth-century theologian Gregory of Nazianzus put it like this: "I cannot think on the one without quickly being circled by the splendour of the three; nor can I discern the three without being straightway carried back to the one".[1]

True Christian spirituality involves a constant movement from the one to the three and the three to the one. We need to train our hearts to think of the three Persons and how we relate to each of them distinctly. But at the same time we need to train ourselves to think of the three as one, so that to relate to one person is to encounter the other two.

2. WE CAN KNOW *MORE* OF GOD: THE PRINCIPLE OF UNION AND COMMUNION

The life of Moses was far from exemplary. But for one moment alone he's my hero.

God had rescued his people from slavery in Egypt. Now in the wilderness they make a calf out of gold and worship it instead of God (Exodus 32 v 1-6). Even so, God reiterates his promise to give them the land of Canaan. "But," he adds, "I will not go with you, because you are a stiff-necked people and I might destroy you on the way" (Exodus 33 v 3).

Think about that offer for a moment. The people can have the blessings of God without the demands of his holy presence. Imagine you were offered a ticket to heaven without the need to be holy. Would you take that offer?

This is what Moses says in response:

If your Presence does not go with us, do not send us up from here. How will anyone know that you are pleased with me and with your people unless you go with us? What

> *else will distinguish me and your people from all the other*
> *people on the face of the earth?*   *(Exodus 33 v 15-16)*

It's an extraordinary response. In some ways Moses is offered the goal of his life's work and he can have it without the obligation of being God's distinctive people. But
knowing God and being his people is what really matters
to Moses. God offers Moses everything without God, but
Moses doesn't want everything. He wants God. And so he
declines the offer. The blessings of the promised land are
secondary to the true blessing which is God himself. We are
not only saved *from* sin; we are saved *for* God.

The Christian life involves a living, felt experience of
God. There is a real relating: a two-way relationship with
giving and receiving, being loved and loving. Christianity
is not just truths about God that we should believe, or a
lifestyle that we should adopt. It's a real two-way relationship—a relationship that we experience here and now. In
the past Christians spoke of this relationship as "communion with God". Today we normally use the word "communion" just to refer to the Lord's Supper. But they used it
more generally to talk about our experience of God (including at the Lord's Supper).

This is where our second principle comes in: our unity
with God in Christ (which is all God's work) is the basis of
our community with God in experience (which is a two-way
relationship). Or more simply, our *union with God* is the basis
of our *communion with God*.

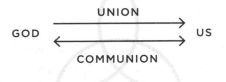

This principle protects us from two contrasting dangers. The first is thinking that our relationship with God is something we achieve. If we devote ourselves to prayer or learn techniques of meditation or work hard in his service then, we might suppose, we can truly know God. But union with God is one-way traffic. It's based entirely on God's grace. It starts with the Father's loving choice. It's achieved through the work of the Son. And it's applied to each of us through the Spirit. So it's not something we achieve at all. It's not even something to which we contribute. It's a gift God gives us in his love. The action is all one-way.

Maybe you've never had a sense of relating to God. That could be because you've never entrusted yourself to Christ. Jesus says, "I am the way and the truth and the life. No one comes to the Father except through me" (John 14 v 6). There's no way of relating to God other than through Jesus.

The second danger is settling for little—little of God.

My mother has been a Christian for almost 60 years. Recently she told me, "Jesus is more precious to me than ever before". The month before she had said, "Your father and I have had more times of blessing reading the Bible this year than at any other point in our lives". Sixty years on from her conversion, my mother is enjoying more of God than ever.

You, too, can know more of God. God has saved us so that we might enjoy a relationship with him—and this relationship with God is two-way. God relates to us and in return we relate to God. So we contribute to the relationship. What we do affects our experience of God.

Imagine two sons. Jack makes breakfast for his father every day and they chat for half an hour while they eat it together. Later in the day Jack and his father hang out together—flying a kite, playing football, reading a book. Meanwhile Jack's older brother, Phil, is embarrassed by his father. Phil stays in his room all day with his music turned up loud. On the rare occasions when Phil communicates with his father, it normally takes the form of dismissive grunts.

How many sons does the father have? The answer, of course, is two. And what did they do to become sons? Nothing. They were simply born as sons. But only Jack enjoys being a son. Only Jack experiences a good relationship with his father.

Praying and reading your Bible won't make you more Christian. And not doing these things won't make you less of a Christian. Somewhat like Jack and Phil, we become children of our heavenly Father by being born—the difference being that Christians are born *again*. We're saved by grace alone through faith in Christ. Our status as God's children is a gift. But how much we enjoy that communion depends on what we do. Paul neatly captured this dynamic when he said, "I press on to take hold of that for which Christ Jesus took hold of me" (Philippians 3 v 12).

DOES WHAT WE DO MATTER?

Grasping this distinction between union and communion protects us from thinking our actions make all the difference on the one hand and thinking our actions make no difference on the other hand.

- Our actions don't make us Christians or make us more of a Christian or keep us as Christians—for our union with God is all his work.
- Our actions do make a difference to our *enjoyment* of God—for our communion with God (our enjoyment of our union with God) involves a two-way relationship.

This is why, even if you're a Christian, your relationship with God can feel weak when you neglect that relationship. And yet at the same time, this is why you can always affirm that your *union* with God is based on the rock-solid ground of Christ's finished work. However much you mess up or neglect your communion with God, you can always start again because you're always united to God in Christ.

We're going to focus on our *communion* with God—on how we can enjoy a living relationship with God. But we must never forget that the foundation of our communion with God is our *union* with God in Christ. The wonder of God's grace is that our relationship with him is not something we have to achieve. It's a gift from beginning to end.

PUTTING IT INTO PRACTICE

When I was young I used to practise batting. I was practising to play cricket, but I'm sure it's the same for baseball or tennis. I would throw a ball against a wall and then hit it with a stick as it returned. Sometimes I used a proper bat, but that was too easy. I was stretching myself so that when I went back to a normal cricket bat, I would be hitting the ball from the centre of the bat. I did this again and again and again. I'm sure it drove my mother mad.

Each chapter of this book ends with a simple step you can take. Think of these steps as the equivalent of throwing a ball against a wall. Some of these actions might feel a little strange at first. But they'll strengthen your spiritual muscles and develop your spiritual instincts.

Or think of it like this. If you're driving at 100 mph, and then you cover your speedometer and try to decelerate to 20 mph, what speed would you actually level out at? For most people the answer would probably be 40-50 mph. Driving at 100 mph alters your perception of "normal" speed.

None of these steps are complicated or hard. But some might feel a little strange or somewhat intense. They might feel like driving at 100 mph. But the aim is that when you stop doing them in a focused way, your normal spiritual "speed" will be 50 mph instead of 20 mph. Talking to God as you drive to work, for example, might feel strange. And doing it during every journey every day for a week will definitely feel intense. But afterwards, it will hopefully become a more natural thing for you. You may find it's much more normal to talk to God or think of God in situations where once you would not have done so.

The action for this chapter is to pray each day for a week to the Father and then to the Son and then to the Spirit. In the New Testament, prayer is normally addressed to the Father through the Son with the help of the Holy Spirit. Normally, but not always. Since praying to the Father is the norm in the New Testament, this should be the norm for our prayers. But Jesus and the Spirit are no less God than the Father, and therefore they can hear and answer prayer. Although there are no clear examples of people praying to the Spirit in the Bible, Stephen prays to Jesus in Acts 7 v 59. So Christians throughout the centuries have also prayed to Jesus and the Spirit as well as to the Father. A famous ninth-century hymn begins:

> *Come, Holy Ghost, Creator, come*
> *From thy bright heav'nly throne;*
> *Come, take possession of our souls,*
> *And make them all thine own.*

It was translated by the Reformer Martin Luther to be sung on the Day of Pentecost. Likewise, the Puritan theologian John Owen says, "The *divine nature* is the reason and cause of all worship; so that it is impossible to *worship any one* Person, and not worship the *whole* Trinity".[2] So he argues that we can pray to the Son and to the Spirit. And praying to the Son and the Spirit is a helpful way of reflecting on their distinctive roles in our lives.

ACTION

Each day for a week spend some time praying to the Father and then to the Son and then to the Spirit. In each case, offer praise or make requests that are particularly related to that Person's distinctive role in your life.

REFLECTION QUESTIONS

- With which member of the Trinity do you have the strongest sense of a lived, experienced relationship?
- What happens if we think of God's oneness to the exclusion of the three Persons?
- What happens if we think of the three Persons to the exclusion of God's unity?
- Do you ever find talk of spirituality or communion with God intimidating? What comfort is there in the principles of union and communion?
- What happens if we think our union with God involves our activity? What happens if we think our communion with God doesn't involve our activity?

2 JOY

Do you want more of God? Do you want to enjoy him? We all know how we're *supposed* to answer those questions. But let's be honest. We're not always sure whether we want to spend more time hanging out with God. There are often other things we'd rather be doing.

Or let's put the question like this: *do you like God?* Perhaps you find that an odd question. We know we're supposed to love God. But liking God? Here's the strange thing. Normally we're pretty adept at deciding whether we like someone. After a few minutes of meeting someone, we quickly form an impression of whether we like them or not. How is it, then, that some of us have known God for years without ever deciding whether we like him? It might be because we think of God as an impersonal force or a set of ideas or a theological system rather than three Persons with whom we have a relationship.

Or it may be that you think of God as cold, distant and aloof. Many Christians start by thinking of God as only a ruler or judge. And, no matter how hard we try, we suppose we'll always be a disappointment to him. It's certainly true that God is King and Judge. But if that's the only way you think about God, then while you might respect such a God, you're not going to like him. We can end up thinking of God as a lonely old man who would rather not be disturbed.

Or it may be that you feel somewhat numb towards God. You agree with Christian truth. But you're not sure that you *feel* it. You see other people excited, lifting their hands in joy, with smiles on their faces—and you feel nothing. All this talk of enjoying God feels a bit intimidating.

Or maybe you really do have a sense of living in relationship with God. You enjoy his presence and feel his touch in your life. But you want more. "You have tasted that the Lord is good," as 1 Peter 2 v 3 puts it. But that's just whetted your appetite to enjoy him more.

Whether you pursue more of God depends on what you think of him. It depends on whether you think a relationship with God is worth pursuing.

There was no doubt in Paul's mind about the answer to that question. What was the goal of his ministry? What was he trying to do as he plodded around the Mediterranean, risking shipwreck, being imprisoned, facing down riots? The answer is: he was trying to bring people *joy*. He tells the church in Corinth, "We work with you for your joy, because it is by faith you stand firm" (2 Corinthians 1 v 24). He says something similar to the church in Philippi: "I will continue with all of you for your progress and joy in the faith" (Philippians 1 v 25). The goal of Paul's ministry was that people might experience joy.

In both these verses joy has something to do with faith. That's because this joy is not something we experience as a result of happy circumstances. It's not that Paul wants us all sitting on the beach with a cold drink in our hands. After all, Paul himself was in prison facing possible execution when he wrote to the Philippians. So this joy is something we can experience *despite* our circumstances.

Paul once described himself as "having nothing, and yet possessing everything" (2 Corinthians 6 v 10). A few lines later he adds, "In all our troubles my joy knows no bounds" (2 Corinthians 7 v 4). How can we have nothing *and* possess everything? How can we have troubles *and* boundless joy? The answer is that faith looks beyond our circumstances to our relationship with God.

Christianity is about a relationship with God, and it is about a relationship with God that brings joy.

Here are some of the benefits of enjoying a relationship with God:

ENJOYING GOD HELPS US OVERCOME TEMPTATION

Sin is a rival to God. Temptation always presents us with a choice between finding joy in God and in the pleasures of sin. The Bible talks about the heart as the driver of our behaviour. We always do what we want. If we're enjoying God, then sin will feel like the poor substitute that it is.

ENJOYING GOD HELPS US ENDURE SUFFERING

Suffering involves loss—loss of health, income, status, love. Those losses are real and painful. But time and again I see people who experience God coping better with such losses. Why? Because we never lose God. Nothing can separate us from his love. When other things are stripped away, we're always left with God, and he is enough.

ENJOYING GOD HELPS TO ENERGISE OUR SERVICE

One of the most diligent workers described in the Bible is the elder brother in the parable of the prodigal son (Luke 15 v 11-32). But one evening his faithful service is exposed for what it is: self-service. It turns out he was never really working for his father, but always for his own reward. He sees himself as a slave rather than as a son. Compare this to another son:

Jesus. Jesus serves as the Son. He went to the cross "for the joy that was set before him" (Hebrews 12 v 2). If you feel like a slave of a distant God who demands your obedience, then your service will always feel like hard work and be characterised by joyless duty. But if you feel like a child of the God who has poured out his love on you, then your service will be willing, full and joyous. You will delight to please your Father rather than feeling obliged to obey your master.

ENJOYING GOD HELPS OUR VIBRANT WITNESS

I'm a Dad and one of my Dad-duties is to insist everyone carefully rolls up the toothpaste tube to extract the last possible spot of toothpaste. It's there in the Dad-manual of pointless Dad-moans. This is how my evangelism often feels. I screw myself up and then reluctantly squeeze out a little dollop of gospel. No one ever seems very impressed.

Yet everyone is an evangelist for the things they love. People will extol the virtues of their favourite sports team or TV show or new boyfriend. And this enthusiasm is infectious. The more we experience a relationship with God and find joy in him, the more our evangelism will be enthusiastic and infectious. It will stop being an awkward exercise imposed on conversation as an act of duty. Instead, as an overflow of full hearts, we will speak enthusiastically of the One we love. Instead of being like nearly empty toothpaste tubes, we'll become champagne bottles, waiting to explode, fizzing and bubbling over.

ENJOYING GOD HELPS TO EMPOWER SACRIFICE

Imagine your church is full of people who say, "Nothing compares with knowing Christ. I'll happily give up my time, money, status, home, future and comfort to serve the gospel." What could we not achieve with people who live like that? Yet this is what Paul said: "I consider everything a loss because of the surpassing worth of knowing Christ Jesus my Lord, for whose sake I have lost all things. I consider them garbage, that I may gain Christ." (Philippians 3 v 8)

Jesus once told a short parable:

> *The kingdom of heaven is like treasure hidden in a field.*
> *When a man found it, he hid it again, and then in his joy*
> *went and sold all he had and bought that field.*
>
> *(Matthew 13 v 44)*

God himself is that treasure. The more we know God, the more willing we'll be to give up everything else. And notice that the man in the parable sells all he has "in his joy". Giving up stuff doesn't normally sound like a fun thing to do. But here's what I've found: most of the significant sacrifices I've made in my life didn't feel like sacrifices at the time. They felt like the obvious thing to do to pursue God and his glory. Sacrifice becomes an opportunity to express our delight in God. What we give up seems small in comparison to what we're gaining.

These are some of the things that are created in our lives when we are relating to God and finding joy in him. Let's flip them around and turn them into a diagnostic tool. Ask yourself if any of the following statements are true of you.

- You often succumb to temptation.
- Suffering and loss fill you with fear.
- Your service feels like drudgery.
- Your witness feels like duty.
- Your sacrifices feel like sacrifices.

If any of these are true, then this is likely to be a sign that you are not finding joy in God as you could.

ENJOYING GOD FOR GOD'S SAKE

And yet… none of these things are the primary reason to pursue a relationship with God. We pursue joy in God for *God's sake,* because he is the source of joy.

Imagine you meet me one morning and I seem cheerful. I'm English so it's hard to tell when I'm happy! But for the sake of the illustration imagine you can. "What's up with you?" you ask. "Why are you so cheerful?" How would you expect me to reply? Suppose I say, "I've decided to be cheerful this morning because it has certain psychological benefits". That would be an odd reply! I'm much more likely to say (as I often do), "The sun is shining, the birds are singing and life is good". And the reason Christians should be joyful is not the secondary (though significant) benefits that being joyful brings, but because we have reasons to be joyful. And the number one reason is God himself. We have God: all that he is to us and all that he does for us.

The German theologian and Reformer Martin Luther loved to describe salvation as a marriage:

> *Faith unites the soul with Christ in the same way that a bride is united with a bridegroom. As a result they come to hold all things in common, the good as well as the bad … Our sins, death and damnation now belong to Christ, while his grace, life and salvation are now ours. For if Christ is a husband, he must take on himself the things which belong to his bride and he must give to her the things that are his. Not only that, he also gives us himself.*[3]

Don't miss that punch line: "He also gives us himself". On her wedding day a bride may receive wealth, status, property and privilege from her new husband. She might be delighted to have access to his DVD collection. She might be excited about moving into her new home. She might be glad to have her name added to his bank account. But what she really wants is him. There are so many blessings that flow from being a Christian, but the real blessing is Christ. Christ is himself his own reward.

There's a danger of making the pursuit of joy a work we must perform. "As if the Christian life wasn't hard enough already," you may be thinking, "now I not only have to obey God's law, but I have to be cheerful about it! Now I have to work hard at 'doing' joy. Now I've somehow got to 'experience' God." It's not like that at all. That's like telling a child they must try very hard to eat chocolate. We give children *permission* to eat chocolate rather than *commands* to do so! For otherwise their pursuit of joy in chocolate would be unrestrained.

Commanding someone to rejoice might seem perverse. But that's what Paul does when he writes to the Philippians. "Rejoice in the Lord always. I will say it again: rejoice!" (Philippians 4 v 4). How can an emotion be commanded? Surely it's the equivalent of telling your child to stop feeling hungry. But Paul doesn't just command us to rejoice. He tells us to rejoice *in the Lord*. We obey the command to rejoice not by drawing up from within ourselves feelings of joy. In any given situation there may be all sorts of good reasons why we don't feel joyful. But we always have a reason for joy that surpasses everything else and that reason is Jesus. You might not tell your child to stop feeling hungry. But you might well say, "Make yourself a sandwich". If you're hungry, then feast on something good. If you lack joy, then feast on *someone* good—Jesus.

For many years I started my day by eating breakfast cereal with milk and a sprinkling of sugar. I found that by mid-morning I was hungry again. Biscuit time! Sugar makes you feel full, but quickly that feeling fades. More recently I've switched to porridge or oatmeal. Oats release their

energy slowly and so my morning porridge easily sees me
through to lunch without any hunger pangs. Many of us
opt for quick-fix sources of joy. We look for joy in status,
possessions, romance, career, sex or holidays. They're like
sugary snacks. They fill you up quickly, but it doesn't last.
Meanwhile Jesus says, "I am the bread of life. Whoever
comes to me will never go hungry, and whoever believes in
me will never be thirsty" (John 6 v 35).

God didn't create the world because he needed love or
wanted cheering up. He's the triune God, who lives eternally in a community of love and mutual delight. Father, Son
and Spirit have all the joy they could ever want and in a far
richer, purer form than we could ever provide. So why did
God create the world when he didn't have to? The answer is
grace—uncompelled, unmerited grace. "He must have created us not to *get* joy, but to *give* it."[4]

THE OBSERVER'S BOOK OF GOD

She smiled at me. It was a smile that said, "I know you mean
well, but I've heard that a hundred times before". She'd
just been describing the struggles of serving with a small
church-planting team as a single woman. One family was
away; another was unwell—it had been a lonely week. So I
told her that, when things are tough, we can always turn to
Christ. "We can always find joy in Christ—and our circumstances don't change that." She smiled.

Perhaps you can see the benefits that finding joy would
bring to your life. Perhaps you agree with the notion that
joy is found in God. But it seems so theoretical. Joy in God
seems a distant prospect. In the new creation we'll experience joy in God because we'll see him face to face. But in
the meantime, an experience of God seems notional and joy
seems elusive. What does a living, day-to-day experience of
the living God look like?

I grew up on the Observer's Books—*The Observer's Book of Wild Flowers, The Observer's Book of Butterflies, The Observer's Book of Geology.* Each book listed the main variations of their theme so that you, the reader—the observer—could spot them. Their postcard-sized, hardback format was part of a golden age of British design. In all there were one hundred books in the series, covering everything from canals to firearms to opera.

I still have my copy of *The Observer's Book of Birds,* written by Vere Benson of "The Bird-Lovers' League". The first entry is a magpie. "This handsome bird is easily distinguished by its glossy black and white plumage and long tail." Equipped with my Observer's Book and binoculars, off I went into the countryside to identify the birdlife of the North Downs in southern England.

In a similar way, this book is the "Observer's Book" of God. It identifies the main ways in which God interacts with us each day. It doesn't describe amazing spiritual experiences that seem remote from your experience. It doesn't outline spiritual disciplines for you to master or spiritual gifts for you to "claim". It's not a book about what you need to achieve. It's about what God has achieved in Christ. It's a book about grace, about how God in his kindness invites us to share in the delight of the Father in the Son and the Son in the Father through the Holy Spirit. It's a spotter's guide to all the very ordinary ways in which that happens every day.

Relating to each Person of the Trinity involves opening our eyes to the work of each in our day-to-day lives. This is an act of faith. When I sit down to eat a lovely meal, it's easy to attribute it to the provision of my local supermarket or my wife's wonderful cooking. And of course both of these are true explanations. But faith recognises my meal as more than this. Faith sees it as a gift from my heavenly Father. Or what about some bad news? It's easy to treat bad news as a disaster. But faith recognises that it's part of my Father's plan to make me more like his Son. So faith then enables me to respond to God the Father—to offer a prayer of thanks for the meal or to accept problems as my Father's means of transforming my heart. This is how the French theologian and Reformer John Calvin puts it:

> *Whatever shall happen prosperously and according to the desire of his heart, God's servant will attribute wholly to God, whether he feels God's beneficence through the ministry of men, or has been helped by inanimate creatures. For thus he will reason in his mind: surely it is the Lord who has inclined their hearts to me, who has so bound them to me that they should become the instruments of his kindness towards me.*[5]

My wife and I have an allotment. An allotment is a strange British institution in which people can rent a pocket of land to grow vegetables. Recently I was at my allotment waiting for a shed to be delivered. The delivery driver was due to phone to let me know when he would arrive. Time went by and no call came. So I checked my phone. It was dead. That put me in a dilemma. Should I stay in case the shed arrived or go home to plug in the phone and find out what was happening? Neither option felt like a good one. I set off towards my car. Then I changed my mind. Standing by my car, I let out an audible cry of frustration.

At that very moment the delivery driver turned up. We unloaded the shed together while he chatted cheerfully away. Then, as I carried a piece of shed wall over to our allotment, two red kites appeared overhead—that's "kite" as in a bird of prey rather than a children's toy. It was the first time I'd seen red kites over our town.

A delivered shed and two birds in the sky. So what? No big deal. But let's view the scene with the eyes of faith. As I walked back towards my allotment, I had a powerful sense of God's goodness. I wish I could say this was God's answer to my prayer. But I hadn't prayed. I'd simply been grumpy. Now it felt as if God was saying, *In my love I've granted the request you didn't make! Oh, and by the way, here are two kites to give you pleasure.* I had to laugh. It was the most loving of rebukes.

"You hem me in," says Psalm 139 v 5, "behind and before". We sometimes ask God to be present or to act. But all the time God is around us, behind us and before us. It's as if we can't move without bumping into him. What we really need is eyes to see and ears to hear. That's what this book attempts to do for you.

PUTTING IT INTO PRACTICE

Whenever you're alone this week, start a conversation with your heavenly Father. This might mean turning off the car radio or taking off your headphones. Or it might mean putting your headphones on so you're not distracted by the conversations on the bus. If you have a tendency to talk to yourself, then this exercise shouldn't be too hard—just direct that internal monologue towards God.

It doesn't matter what you say. Just talk about whatever you're thinking about. Talk about the day ahead or the day that's past. Talk about the things that are exciting you or worrying you or annoying you. Tell God about your day-dreams. The aim is to reinforce the idea that we have a two-way relationship with God. At any time and in any place, we can relate to God.

ACTION

Whenever you're alone this week, start a conversation with your heavenly Father in which you talk to him about whatever is on your mind.

REFLECTION QUESTIONS

- The previous chapter ended with a challenge to pray to the Father, to the Son and to the Spirit. How have you got on?
- Do you like God? Does it seem like an odd question?
- How has enjoying God helped you overcome temptation or endure suffering? How has it energised service, witness and sacrifice?
- The Bible commands us to rejoice. But how is joy something we can be commanded to have?
- What might it mean for you to pursue other people's joy in Christ (as Paul did)?
- How have you observed God at work in your life over the past 24 hours?

IN EVERY PLEASURE
WE CAN ENJOY
THE FATHER'S GENEROSITY

God has forgiven us, redeemed us and justified us through Christ. But is it enough?

Maybe it's enough for you. After all, it is amazing! But it's not enough for God. He wants more for us and from us.

If that were all God the Father had done, how would we relate to him? I assume we would be eternally grateful. I assume we would want to serve him fully. But it wouldn't create any intimacy. Maybe that's how you feel about God the Father. You honour him, but you don't really love him—not with any real affection. You don't enjoy him.

But listen to what Paul says:

> *In love [God the Father] predestined us for adoption*
> *to sonship through Jesus Christ, in accordance with his*
> *pleasure and will.* *(Ephesians 1 v 5)*

We used to be "sons of disobedience" and "children of wrath" (Ephesians 2 v 2-3, ESV). But now we're sons and daughters of God. We're family. We're loved. "In love he predestined us for adoption," says Paul. "Predestined" simply means "chosen". We were chosen *in* love *for* love. "See what great love the Father has lavished on us, that we should be called children of God! And that is what we are!" (1 John 3 v 1). The author J. I. Packer says:

> *Adoption ... is the highest privilege that the gospel offers: higher even than justification ... In adoption, God takes us into his family and fellowship—he establishes us as his children and heirs. Closeness, affection and generosity are at the heart of the relationship. To be right with God the Judge is a great thing, but to be loved and cared for by God the Father is a greater.*[6]

IT STARTS WITH LOVE

You might believe all this, but still think of God as "the reluctant Father" who has to be won over by Jesus. I wonder if you assume God is often displeased with you—perhaps even suspicious of you. You realise you don't live as you should and so you wonder if God really loves you. Maybe you think God is gracious because that's what God is supposed to be, but you assume there's no delight in it for him, no pleasure, no affection. At best he tolerates you. More often he's frustrated with you. John Owen says some believers "are afraid to have good thoughts of God".[7]

But the Father chose us "before the creation of the world". "In love [God the Father] predestined us for adoption" (Ephesians 1 v 4-5). *It all begins with the Father's love.* The Father is not reluctant. Quite the opposite: it all starts with his love.

LOVED IN CHRIST

But it gets even better. Ephesians 1 v 5 says: "In love he predestined us for adoption to sonship *through Jesus Christ*". God the Father relates to us *in Christ.* Verse 6 says the Father has "freely given us [this grace of adoption] *in the One he loves*". We are in his Son. The Father loves his Son and now he loves us in his Son. In other words, the Father loves us with the same love that he has for his own Son.

When did God become a Father? It's a trick question! He's always been a Father. Paul begins in verse 3 with praise "to the God and Father of our Lord Jesus Christ". So God is not *like* a father. He *is* a Father. When we say "God is a rock" we're using a *metaphor*. There are certain features of rocks that are similar to certain features of God (they both make reliable foundations). But God isn't a piece of inanimate stone. But it's a different story when we speak of God as Father. "Father" is not a metaphor. We're not saying God is a bit like human fathers. Throughout all eternity God is Father because eternally he has a Son. God is the pattern for true fatherhood. This is really important for some people. Your experience of your human father may be very mixed: he may have been distant, harsh or even abusive—or simply not there. But that's not what God is like. God is the loving Father you've always wished you had.

Christians speak of the Son as "eternally begotten" by the Father. There wasn't a moment in time when the Father brought the Son into existence. The Father eternally gives life to the Son and eternally loves the Son. Just as the sun constantly pours out light and heat, so life and love constantly radiate out from the Father to the Son. And now they radiate out to us. Our job is to go sunbathing in the Father's love! Close your eyes, sit back in your chair and feel the warmth of his love on your skin.

YOU ARE THE FATHER'S PLEASURE

It's the Father's pleasure to adopt us. You are his pleasure. Paul says our adoption was "in accordance with his pleasure and will" (Ephesians 1 v 5). The Puritan Richard Sibbes says, "What a comfort is this, that seeing God's love rests on Christ, as well pleased in him, we may gather that he is as well pleased with us, if we be in Christ!"[8] If you're in Christ, you always bring pleasure to the Father. He sees you and smiles with delight.

At the 2012 Olympics, the South African swimmer Chad le Clos won a gold medal. His father, Bert le Clos, was famously interviewed afterwards. His joy was uncontained. "Look at my boy," he kept saying. "He's so beautiful." God the Father has created us so he could say to us, "This is my beloved Son in whom I am well pleased". But more than that, God the Father saves us so we can share that love. In Christ he says *of us*, "This is my beloved child in whom I am well pleased". He adopts us into his family. He's not just the Father of Jesus. We can call him *"our* Father".

"The LORD your God is with you, the Mighty Warrior who saves," says Zephaniah 3 v 17. "He will take great delight in you; in his love he will no longer rebuke you, but will rejoice over you with singing." God rejoices over you with singing. As you read your Bible and as you reflect on your life, listen out for the echo of the Father's song. Look for the signs of his love. Rejoice in that love. Welcome that love.

John Owen said this: "The greatest sorrow and burden you can lay on the Father, the greatest unkindness you can do to him, is…" How would you complete this sentence? Not to love him? Not to live a godly life? Not to serve others? Owen said, "You can no way more trouble or burden the Father, than by your unkindness in not believing in his love".[9] This is how editor R. J. K. Law restates it: "The greatest sorrow and burden you can lay on the Father, the greatest unkindness you can do to him, is *not to believe that he loves you.*"[10]

Why? Because the whole plan of salvation has as its goal your adoption as God's beloved child. God sent his Son, condemned his Son and abandoned his Son on the cross so you could come close—so you could be his child. To doubt his love, to reject his family, to stand at a distance—that is the greatest unkindness you can show to God.

First and foremost, you have communion with the Father by believing he loves you.

A FATHERED WORLD

What does this mean day to day? Think back over the past week at all the good things you've enjoyed—the food, the achievements, the family, the entertainment. Think of the beauty, the laughter, the tears, the love. These are all signs of your Father's care. One way we relate to the Father—one way we enjoy him—is to see these things as his gifts.

In Luke 12, Jesus invites us not to worry:

> *[22] Therefore I tell you, do not worry about your life, what you will eat; or about your body, what you will wear. [23] For life is more than food, and the body more than clothes. [24] Consider the ravens: they do not sow or reap, they have no storeroom or barn; yet God feeds them. And how much more valuable you are than birds! [25] Who of you by worrying can add a single hour to your life? [26] Since you cannot do this very little thing, why do you worry about the rest?*
>
> *[27] "Consider how the wild flowers grow. They do not labour or spin. Yet I tell you, not even Solomon in all his splendour was dressed like one of these. [28] If that is how God clothes the grass of the field, which is here today, and tomorrow is thrown into the fire, how much more will he clothe you—you of little faith! [29] And do not set your heart on what you will eat or drink; do not worry about it. [30] For the pagan world runs after all such things, and your*

Father knows that you need them. [31] But seek his kingdom, and these things will be given to you as well.

(Luke 12 v 22-31)

Twice Jesus invites us to "consider" the world around us. We're to consider the ravens (v 24) and we're to consider the wild flowers (v 27). The point is clear: we don't need to worry, because the world is full of signs of our Father's intimate involvement. *We live in a fathered world.*

One of the characteristics of modern culture is that people only see natural causes. We find it hard to imagine anything beyond the world around us. It's as if we're looking at a picture and seeing only what's within the frame. We've lost the ability to recognise the hand of the artist. Any causes from outside the frame are dismissed.[11] When Christians insist that God sometimes bursts into the frame by performing miracles, we're actually assuming we're enclosed by the frame—that the world is full of natural causes with just a few occasional miraculous causes. We're conceding that God only occasionally dabbles in our lives.

But in fact, *everything* is an act of God. Sometimes God acts directly (in what we call miracles) and sometimes God acts indirectly through intermediate causes (which we call natural causes). But everywhere our heavenly Father is at work. The postman who delivers a comforting letter is an agent of God, even if they are unwitting partners with God. The farmer, the miller, the baker, the shopkeeper—or their industrial equivalents—are agents of God's kindness, used by God to gift us food.

Living within the frame means we only occasionally see God at work because we only see him in the extraordinary. But remove the frame and suddenly the world lights up. Suddenly divine generosity can now be seen wherever you look. Listen to Ruth, the central character of Marilynne Robinson's novel *Housekeeping*, describing her grandmother's care of her three daughters after the untimely death of their father:

> *She had always known a thousand ways to circle them all around with what must have seemed like grace. She knew a thousand songs. Her bread was tender and her jelly was tart, and on rainy days she made cookies and applesauce. In the summer she kept roses in a vase on the piano, huge, pungent roses, and when the blooms ripened and the petals fell, she put them in a tall Chinese jar, with cloves and thyme and sticks of cinnamon. Her children slept on starched sheets under layers of quilts, and in the morning her curtains filled with light the way sails fill with wind.*[12]

God has a thousand ways to circle us around with his grace (and they include a grandmother's care).

You see the birds and enjoy their song. What's the explanation? How do you see it? There are all sorts of natural explanations—evolutionary drives, natural instincts, territorial defence. Jesus invites us to see the intimate involvement of God—to see a fathered world. You see the flowers. They're so beautiful. And yet they are here today and gone tomorrow (Luke 12 v 28). This is disposable art of the highest order! What's the explanation? What do you see? There are all sorts of natural explanations—seeds, genetics, photosynthesis. Jesus invites us to see the intimate involvement of God—to see a fathered world. The 19th-century preacher Charles Spurgeon says:

> *How often Luther liked to talk about the birds and the way God cares for them! When he was full of his anxieties, he used to constantly envy the birds because they led so free and happy a life. He talks of Dr Sparrow, Dr Thrush and others that used to come and talk to*

Dr Luther and tell him many a good thing! You know,
brothers and sisters, the birds out in the open, yonder,
cared for by God, fare far better than those that are cared
for by man.[13]

The lie of the serpent in the Garden of Eden was that God
is an uncaring Father and so we should go it alone. Satan
didn't dispute the existence of God nor his power. The lie
was that God doesn't care. All the evidence was to the con-
trary. God had placed Adam and Eve in a place of security
and plenty—and given them the fruit of every tree except
one. His provision was complete. Yet humanity believed the
lie that God is distant and uncaring. We still do. Still today,
says Jesus, our problem is that we lack faith (v 28). We don't
believe God cares. We think of him as distant. We see this
world as unfathered.

Imagine a young child having a nightmare. The monsters
are closing in and about to pounce. Then the child becomes
aware of being shaken. They open their eyes and see the
concerned face of their father. Suddenly everything is OK
and they can smile again. Our problem is that we often
think the threats in our lives are reality and the promises of
God are like a dream world. But many of the threats we face
are a dream. We play out the "what ifs" and "maybes" in
our mind, creating all sorts of frightening possibilities. But
they're not real. They exist only in our imagination. Other
problems are all too real. But they're not the *whole* truth. We
need to be shaken by God's word out of the dreamland in
which God is absent and into the real world, the fathered
world. We need to open the eyes of faith and see the smile
of our heavenly Father.

John Owen encourages us to use our imaginations. He
asks us to picture anything with "a loving and tender nature
in the world," and then imagine it with all the imperfections

taken away. In this way we begin to get a picture of the Father's love. "He is as a father, a mother, a shepherd, a hen over chickens." All these serve as pointers to the source of love which is the love of the Father.[14]

WE RESPOND BY RECEIVING OUR BLESSINGS AS HIS GIFT

This world is a magical place. God's verdict on his world: "God saw all that he had made, and it was *very good*" (Genesis 1 v 31). It's a world of wonders. We live in a world of oak trees, a thousand varieties of rice, Jane Austen's novels, neon lights, past participles, space probes, snails, curry. Pick up anything—anything—and you will hold in your hand a thing of wonder!

Think about a glass of water. The simplest of things, yet all life depends on it. We drink water. Wash in it. Swim in it. Play with it. You can have water fights. We live in a world of water pistols. Why? Just so we can have fun. And it rains on you. We live in a world in which water just falls from the sky. Is that not the most extraordinary thing? Don't moan about a rainy day. Which of us would have designed a world in which water falls out of the sky?

You have no reason ever to be bored—not in *God's* world. We live in a world with an excess of beauty, a redundancy of beauty.

Think about a leaf. Every leaf is unique. God could have made a world in which every leaf was the same. It would have saved him a lot of bother. He could have made a world in which leaves were like plastic cups, punched out to the same design. But every leaf is handmade. And every leaf is a thing of exquisite beauty. The way the veins snake under the surface when you hold it up to light. What's more, each year half of them transform from a translucent green into rich, deep reds, browns and yellows. And then think of a forest!

There are millions of leaves, each one unique and each one a thing of beauty. If you went to your local woods and tried to appreciate every leaf, it would take you a lifetime. And yet each spring God starts the process all over again. He says to himself, *That was great. Let's do it again.*

Every leaf is different. Every snowflake is different. Every fingerprint is different. God paints swirls on every fingerprint and every one is unique. Why? It makes no sense. The vast majority of this beauty goes unnoticed, unremarked and unappreciated. Except by God. He's doing it for his own pleasure and his own glory. God is having a ball. In Proverbs 8 v 30-31, Wisdom speaks as if it's a person. This is Jesus, our true Wisdom. Jesus says that when God was creating the world, "Then I was constantly at his side. I was filled with delight day after day, rejoicing always in his presence, rejoicing in his whole world and delighting in the human race." His days are filled with delight as he enjoys the beauty of each leaf and each life.

In the book *Charlie and the Chocolate Factory*, Willy Wonka issues five golden tickets so that five lucky winners can enter his amazing chocolate factory. God has issued at least seven billion golden tickets, and you're one of those lucky recipients. You've been chosen to enter God's amazing world.

- A world where water falls out of the sky.
- A world where ants build hills.
- A world where water melts, drips, freezes again and makes icicles—genius!
- A world with magnetic poles so compasses point north.
- A world in which a string sounds a note and then when you halve the string's length, it sounds the same note a perfect octave higher—what are the chances?
- A world in which you can skim stones across water—it's magical.

- A world of puns and rhymes and rhythm and alliteration—a world in which words are fun.
- A world in which music can make you cry.

You have no reason to be bored in *God's* world.

GRATITUDE LEADS US CLOSER TO GOD

Dave is an army officer who's sometimes away on deployment or exercise. When he's away he often sends his wife, Suzy, flowers as a sign of his love. It would be perverse for Suzy to complain about Dave's lack of care while praising the florists who deliver her flowers. God uses means to deliver his gifts to us. And it's right to thank those who are generous towards us (just as I'm sure Suzy thanks the florist who delivers her flowers). But it's God who is the ultimate Giver. And we shouldn't praise the means while thinking of God as distant and uninvolved.

Giving thanks is a powerful act. We all too easily focus on what we lack and feel discontented. A thousand adverts are designed to reinforce that feeling so we buy the products they offer. But gratitude redirects our thoughts away from the trifles that we lack and towards the amazing blessings that are already ours. Sunshine, birdsong and friendship are all waiting to be enjoyed, to be relished—and all without requiring any payment. And that is before we begin to count the blessings that are ours as children of God. The key that unlocks this treasury of joy is gratitude.

Even more significantly, gratitude lifts our eyes from the gift to see the Giver. In other words, gratitude leads back to God. Jesus once encountered ten lepers who cried out to him to have pity on them. Jesus sent them to the priest, the person who could certify that they had been cleansed (Luke 17 v 11-19). As they went they were healed. One of them returned to Jesus, threw himself at his feet and thanked him. At the end of the story all ten lepers were former lepers. But only one was with Jesus. Only one was enjoying communion with Jesus. And what had drawn him back to Jesus was gratitude. Gratitude may not affect our physical location. But it will bring us close to God, the great Giver.

PUTTING IT INTO PRACTICE

All the things we enjoy, says John Calvin, are "ladders by which we may ascend nearer to God". "God," he says, "by his benefits, gently attracts us to himself, giving us a taste of his fatherly sweetness". But Calvin also warns, "There is nothing into which we more easily fall than into a forgetfulness of him, especially when we enjoy peace and comfort".[15]

Think back over the past week at all the good things you have enjoyed. Identify five things to give thanks for. A specific number helps you think harder about how God has been kind to you. Imagine each one being handed to you as a gift from your heavenly Father. One way we relate to the Father is to receive these things as his gifts—to thank him for these things, to look for answers for prayer, to tell other people how he's provided for us, to celebrate every good thing as his provision.

ACTION

*Each day this week pick something that makes you happy and pray: "My Father, thank you for **this** because it's a lovely gift from you."*

MIKE AND EMMA'S MONDAY MORNING

Monday morning. The day had started so well. Still buoyed by yesterday's experience at church, he'd sat down to a bacon sandwich. The kids were playing quietly in the front room. He took Emma a coffee to drink in bed and kissed her gently on the cheek. Outside, the sun was shining and the birds were singing. Could life be any better?

As Mike walks down the road he says, "My Father, thank you for that bacon sandwich. What a treat. This beautiful morning is a lovely gift from you. You're so generous. You've given me a great church and a beautiful family. Help me to see you at work in my day. And thank you for the birds. Even if I didn't praise you, they would go on singing to your glory!"

REFLECTION QUESTIONS

- The previous chapter ended with a challenge to start a conversation with your heavenly Father in which you talk to him about whatever is on your mind. How have you got on?
- How does knowing Jesus change the way we think about God the Father?
- What difference does seeing the world as a fathered world make to our worries? To our pleasures?
- How would your attitude change if you thought of yourself as the winner of a golden ticket giving you access to a world full of wonder?
- Think of one thing in the world that fills you with wonder.

IN EVERY HARDSHIP
WE CAN ENJOY
THE FATHER'S FORMATION

For ten years my friends had been preparing to lead a church-planting team to one of the largest unreached people groups of the world. Then one day they walked into a doctor's consulting room to be told that their unborn baby had a major abnormality and disability. In that moment all their plans were turned upside down. Those plans were not aimed at wealth or security. They had been heading to a dangerous part of the world to serve Christ on the frontline. But not any more. "I don't mind having a disabled child," the father told me. "But it will break my heart to wave goodbye as others go while we stay behind."

What's God doing? It's easy to see how the good things of life might be opportunities to enjoy God. But what about the hardships? What about traffic jams? Screaming babies? Chronic illness? Sleepless nights? Unreasonable bosses? Personal conflict? Broken promises? Nuisance neighbours? Unfulfilled hopes?

Here's the answer of the writer of Hebrews:

*⁵ And have you completely forgotten this word of
encouragement that addresses you as a father addresses his
son? It says,*

> *"My son, do not make light of the Lord's discipline,*
>   *and do not lose heart when he rebukes you,*
> *⁶ because the Lord disciplines the one he loves,*
>   *and he chastens everyone he accepts as his son."*

*⁷ Endure hardship as discipline; God is treating you as
his children. For what children are not disciplined by
their father? ⁸ If you are not disciplined—and everyone
undergoes discipline—then you are not legitimate, not true
sons and daughters at all.*   *(Hebrews 12 v 5-8)*

The writer of Hebrews describes this as a "word of encouragement" (v 5). I firmly believe this is true. Seeing hardship
as God's discipline is revolutionary. It has the potential to
transform our attitude to suffering.

IN EVERY HARDSHIP WE CAN ENJOY THE FATHER'S LOVE

Hebrews gives us a word from our Father (via Proverbs 3
v 11-12): "The Lord disciplines the one he loves, and he
chastens everyone he accepts as his son" (Hebrews 12 v 6).
Hardship is not a sign that God dislikes or disowns us.
Quite the opposite. It's a sign that he loves us and accepts
us as his children. Christ says much the same thing to the
church in Laodicea: "Those whom I love I rebuke and discipline" (Revelation 3 v 19).

At first sight that might seem an unlikely claim. How can
our pain be the product of God's love? The writer draws a
comparison with human fathers: "For what children are not
disciplined by their father? If you are not disciplined—and
everyone undergoes discipline—then you are not legitimate,

not true sons and daughters at all" (Hebrews 12 v 7-8). Disciplining children is hard work. It's often easier just to ignore what your toddler has done or leave your angry teenager holed up in their room. As human parents we often decide to let it go this time round. We don't want a head-to-head confrontation in the supermarket aisle to spoil our comfort or ruin our reputation. But we know that's a selfish attitude. We know we would be sacrificing the long-term nurture of our children for the sake of our short-term convenience. I realise sometimes you have to choose your battles. But the point still stands: in the long run *discipline is an act of love*.

Our heavenly Father is no different. He loves us and therefore he disciplines us. And we can turn this around: if love leads to discipline, then discipline can be a sign of love. That's the point the writer of Hebrews is making: "The Lord disciplines the one he loves" (Hebrews 12 v 6).

For some of us this may be very hard to do, but seeing this world as a fathered world enables us to welcome every hardship as a sign of the Father's love. And that has the power to turn a bad day into a good day. A bad day becomes a day full of God's fatherly discipline, and God's fatherly discipline is a sign of fatherly love.

But we can go further. This passage doesn't come out of the blue. In Hebrews 11 the writer lists many of the great heroes of faith from the Old Testament. He brings that list to a climax with Jesus—"the pioneer and perfecter of faith" (12 v 1-2). The writer's application is this: "Consider him who endured such opposition from sinners, so that you will not grow weary and lose heart" (12 v 3). Jesus is *the* Son. He's God's Son by nature, sharing the very being of God the Father. Yet Jesus the divine Son was disciplined. "Son though he was," says Hebrews 5 v 8, "he learned obedience from what he suffered". The "pioneer" of salvation was made "perfect through what he suffered" (2 v 10). It's not that Jesus was sinful and had to be corrected. Rather, he was *equipped* to be our mediator by suffering with us. Suffering prepared him for the job he had to do.

Now the writer of Hebrews invites us to "consider him" because we, too, are children of God. We're not sons by nature, but we are sons and daughters by adoption. And our suffering is a sign that we're sons like the Son, with a relationship to the Father like the Son's relationship to the Father.

I gripped my daughter tightly in my arms while she fought against me. She cried out in confused protest. How could her father turn so nasty? Meanwhile her mother attempted to spoon evil-tasting liquids down her throat. Imagine the scene. You might well have been tempted to intervene, to rescue this poor girl from the cruelty of her parents. Except of course by now you've worked out that we were administering medicine. Through our apparent cruelty we were imparting health and making her whole. What kind of a father would fight his daughter in this way? A father full of love.

Sometimes God the Father holds us tightly in his grip—so tight it hurts. But it's a sign of his love. With great patience and persistence he's ridding us of the fever of our sin. The author Frederick Leahy says, "God does not punish our sins in a legal sense: that he did fully at Calvary. The chastisements he brings upon his people are to be understood as the loving corrections of a merciful and tender-hearted father."[16]

Suffering can be a means of communion with God, of enjoying our relationship with him. If we receive hardship by faith, it has the power to bring us closer to our heavenly Father. In every adversity we can enjoy the Father's love.

IN EVERY HARDSHIP WE CAN ENJOY THE FATHER'S FORMATION

God has a purpose for our suffering. He's using hardship to shape us and grow us:

> *Moreover, we have all had human fathers who disciplined us and we respected them for it. How much more should we submit to the Father of spirits and live! They disciplined us for a little while as they thought best; but God disciplines us for our good.* (Hebrews 12 v 9-10)

Again, Hebrews draws a parallel between human discipline and divine discipline. Discipline has a purpose. We normally discipline our children so they grow and mature. We want to teach them to have respect for authority and concern for others. Normally. There are other times when we discipline our children because we're frustrated or annoyed. That doesn't usually go well! Sometimes we do our best, but our knowledge is limited. Our children come with their he-said, she-said disputes and we have to arbitrate without really knowing what went on. But in principle at least we recognise that discipline is for a child's good.

Now imagine a perfect Father. A Father who is not reliant on second-hand accounts from sibling rivals. A Father who sees not just our actions but our hearts. A Father with infinite patience who measures his discipline with perfect wisdom. What might that Father achieve? The answer is holiness: "God disciplines us for our good, in order that we may share in his holiness" (Hebrews 12 v 10).

This doesn't mean we have to pretend bad things are good things. Evil is evil. If you're the victim of injustice, you can say it as it is: injustice is wrong. If you're struggling with sickness, you can say it as it is: sickness is a scar on the good world God made. We don't have to pretend bad things are pleasant. "No discipline seems pleasant at the time," says verse 11, "but painful". It's OK to say, "It hurts". Disability, loss, disappointment, pressure—they're all painful.

But in God's hands bad things are also full of purpose. Verse 11 continues, "No discipline seems pleasant at the time, but painful. Later on, however, it produces a harvest of righteousness and peace for those who have been trained by it." We can be confident that God is using this bad thing, even the evil intent of sinful people, for his glory and our good. We see an example of this in the life of Joseph, sold as a slave by his jealous brothers. Looking back on their betrayal, Joseph was able to say to them, "You intended to harm me, but God intended it for good to accomplish what is now being done, the saving of many lives" (Genesis 50 v 20).

The idea that God uses hardship to produce holiness raises a key question: does God's discipline mean we need to change direction or repent of a specific sin? The answer, I think, is: *sometimes, but not often.*

Sometimes God's discipline is a call to repent of a specific sin. For example, some members of the church of Corinth were bringing their social snobbery into the church and despising their fellow Christians. What's more, they used the Lord's Supper—the great symbol of Christian unity—to reinforce these social divisions. They dined in style while the poor went without. Here's Paul verdict: "Those who eat and drink without discerning the body of Christ eat and drink judgment on themselves. That is why many among you are weak and ill, and a number of you have fallen asleep" (1 Corinthians 11 v 29-30). Their sickness is God's discipline on a specific sin and Paul calls them to repent. So sometimes God disciplines us to lead us to repentance.

But this is *not normally* how God's discipline works. Jesus rejects the assumption that every suffering is linked to a specific sin (as the healing of a man born blind in John 9 shows). God's discipline is much broader than simply correction. We mustn't think of a headmaster wielding his cane or handing out lines.

So how do I know if my hardship is a sign that I need to repent? The answer is that the sin will be persistent and it will be clear. God is not waiting, poised to hit out at us every time we put a foot wrong. That's not how the discipline of a loving father works and that's not how God's discipline works. He's not out to get us. He's working for our good. His aim is holiness. And God doesn't play guessing games with us. Sin can blind us, so we may need someone to point it out to us—as Paul did with the Corinthians. But it will become clear if we need to repent of a specific sin.

This means we don't have to tie ourselves up in knots trying to interpret our circumstances. We don't have to be able to say, "This happened because of this". Most of the time we can't.

So how does God's discipline normally work? The writer of Hebrews talks about being "trained" by discipline (12 v 11), and he begins with an image from athletics: "Let us throw off everything that hinders and the sin that so easily entangles. And let us run with perseverance the race marked out for us" (Hebrews 12 v 1). You can't run well if you're wearing a heavy coat or carrying a few extra pounds round your waist. You need a training regime to get you into shape. Or think of a trainer preparing a boxer for a fight: making him lift weights, do endless skipping, press-ups, sit-ups, sparring with him in the ring. Think of Rocky sprinting up the steps of the Philadelphia Museum of Art followed by a swarm of local kids. "Discipline" in this sense is the discipline of an athlete's coach. God's discipline is like a training regime to get us into shape so we can fight the good fight and finish the race (1 Timothy 6 v 12; 2 Timothy 4 v 7).

I recently watched a four-year-old boy clamber up a climbing frame and go over the top with a view to going down the other side. But at the top he froze. He was stuck—too afraid to go on and unable to climb backwards. So he shouted to his dad for help, but his dad said, "You'll be fine". More shouts. More apparent parental indifference.

Eventually the father came and stood beneath his son, ready to catch him. But still he refused to help. In the end his son inched his foot forwards, then switched position and finally made it down again to a shout of approval from his dad. Then the boy did it all over again: climbed up, got stuck at the same spot, more cries for help, more shouts of encouragement. Soon he was doing it with alacrity and confidence. By not going to help his son, the father forced him to learn and gain confidence. Stuck at the top of the climbing frame, shouting for help, the boy may have felt abandoned by his father. But what looked like indifference was in fact a calculated act of training. Sometimes this is how God's discipline works. We may cry out for help and we may feel God is indifferent. But in fact he is teaching us to trust him, to deepen our godliness and refine our faith. And all the time he is ready to catch us if we fall.

Or think of a new employee being given a series of tasks to equip them for their role. Perhaps they receive some instruction—just as Christians do through the preaching of the church. But they'll also be given tasks where they can experience all the challenges of the job. Remember, our discipline as sons and daughters of God is modelled on the perfecting of Jesus the Son (Hebrews 2 v 10; 5 v 8). For Jesus, discipline didn't mean correcting what was wrong, but equipping him for his role. In the same way, God the Father carefully organises all the circumstances of our lives to equip us to trust him and serve him.

HOW WAS YOUR DAY TODAY?

Think about that for a moment. Look back over your day. Everything that has happened was put in place by God the Father for your good and to develop your holiness. Think about activities you planned and events that took you by surprise. Think about what you've enjoyed and what went wrong. The piece of toast that landed butter-side down. The toothpaste down your clean sweater. The milk your child spilled on the carpet. All were part of his tailor-made training regime. This perspective radically alters how we view each moment of our day. Sometimes we're forced to think through the big challenges that life throws our way: things like long-term illness, unemployment or the loss of a child. But we're less used to seeing day-to-day events as part of God's design.

Suppose you hit a traffic jam. It's very easy to get wound up. You worry about a late appointment. You're frustrated by the wasted time. But what happens if you remind yourself, "God hasn't lost control of my life. This is his plan. He's designed this with me in mind. Is this an opportunity to learn something? Is it an opportunity to pray? Is it a God-given moment for reflection on my life or meditation on God's word?" Or maybe you can't identify any purpose in it. But that doesn't mean there isn't one. It's enough for you to trust your Father's care. It's enough for you to pray, "My Father, thank you for this. Please use it to make me more like Jesus."

Paul famously says, "And we know that in all things God works for the good of those who love him". Here is God the Father working in the details of our lives. And what is his purpose? That we might "be conformed to the image of his Son, that he might be the firstborn among many brothers and sisters" (Romans 8 v 28-29). Notice how we've come back round to God as our Father and Jesus as our brother. God uses the hardships of our lives to transform us into the image of his Son so that the Son might have many siblings sharing his experience of being loved by the Father.

God disciplines us to refine our faith, wean us from idols, unsettle our self-reliance, display his power and direct us heavenwards. Above all, he disciplines us so that we turn from futile sources of joy to find true joy in him.

PUTTING IT INTO PRACTICE

How should we respond to the hardships in our lives? Hebrews 12 v 5 gives us two answers: "My son, do not make light of the Lord's discipline, and do not lose heart when he rebukes you."

1. DO NOT MAKE LIGHT OF THE LORD'S DISCIPLINE

We treat God's discipline lightly when we fail to see his hand in our hardship. Too often we see hardship as a problem to be solved or a fact of life to be endured or a disaster without purpose. But verse 7 says, "Endure hardship as *discipline*". In other words, when hardship comes, think of it not only as hardship, but also as discipline. Receive it as a gift from God. Take it seriously as an opportunity to grow.

2. DO NOT LOSE HEART WHEN HE REBUKES YOU

When things are tough, it's easy to assume that God has abandoned us—that he doesn't care or he's given up on us. So don't forget "this word of encouragement that addresses you as a father addresses his sons" (v 5). The writer of Hebrews is giving a different way of interpreting the evidence. That screaming baby or grumpy boss or broken relationship is a sign of God's involvement in our lives. "The Lord disciplines the one he loves, and he chastens everyone he accepts as his son" (v 6). "God is treating you as his children" (v 7). God's discipline in our lives is a sign that we are "true sons and daughters" (v 8).

One final thought: try this thought-experiment with me. Close your eyes and imagine that you're in the passenger seat of a car that is being driven in poor conditions. The rain is falling, the traffic is heavy and it's dark outside. A few years ago I aquaplaned in just such driving conditions, turning the car 180 degrees so I was facing in the wrong direction. So I'm feeling pretty nervous. What about you? Do you feel safe? Of course, the answer depends on how careful and competent your driver is. So think of yourself being carried in your heavenly Father's arms. The journey is your life. Throughout your life you are cocooned in the arms of your Father. And he is the most careful and most competent driver.

Close your eyes again and return to our imaginary car driving in the rain. Become aware of the noise around you: the rumble of the tyres on the road, the splash of the water as other cars pass, perhaps the squeak of the windscreen wipers. Think of that noise as a kind of cocoon in which you are sheltered, a kind of buffer against the world. And then replace that noise with a sense of God's presence. Though the road may be bumpy at times, we can be confident he will bring us safely home to glory.[17]

ACTION

Each time this week that something goes wrong, pray, "My Father, thank you for this. Please use it to make me more like Jesus."

MIKE AND EMMA'S MONDAY MORNING

Mike arrives at the station to find his train has been cancelled. Two train-loads of passengers are now crammed onto the next train and Mike is having to stand. He's given up any hope of reading his book. The guy pushed up against him has clearly not heard of deodorant. The next 40 minutes are not going to be fun.

"Perhaps God thinks I need to learn some patience," Mike thinks to himself. "Or perhaps he's giving me this time to reflect on yesterday's sermon." "My Father," whispers Mike, "thank you for this train. I have no idea what your purpose is in all this. But please use it to make me more like Jesus."

Meanwhile Emma is wiping up milk from the kitchen floor. Sam and Jamie are arguing about socks. And little

Poppy… Where's Poppy? Emma looks up to see the box of cornflakes topple off the kitchen table. "How can a day go so wrong so quickly?" she thinks.

"But God is still good," she tells herself. "Father, I thank you for my day—even though it hasn't started as well as I might have hoped. Give me the strength to remain calm. And please use this day to make me more like Jesus."

REFLECTION QUESTIONS

- The previous chapter ended with a challenge to receive this world as a gift from God through thanksgiving. How have you got on?
- Think about your experience of discipline from your earthly father. How do you think this colours your view of God's discipline?
- Can you look back on a time when God used hardship to make you more like Jesus?
- What might it look like to make light of God's discipline? What might it look like to lose heart? How can we safeguard ourselves from these attitudes?
- When we are faced with suffering, we typically ask ourselves, "What am I going to do?" But take a current struggle and reframe your response by asking, "What does God want me to learn?" or "How does God want me to change?"

IN EVERY PRAYER
WE CAN ENJOY
THE FATHER'S WELCOME

God the Father is kind. "He has shown kindness," says Paul to the people of Lystra, "by giving you rain from heaven and crops in their seasons; he provides you with plenty of food and fills your hearts with joy" (Acts 14 v 17). But his kindness to his people is even richer and fuller. He has shown us "the incomparable riches of his grace, expressed in his kindness to us in Christ Jesus" (Ephesians 2 v 7).

I find the term "kindness" really helpful when I'm thinking about God the Father. "Love" is such a big word and it can embrace a rather formal caring. We could, for example, use it to describe a father who worked hard to provide for his family, but never showed any interest or delight in his children. Maybe this is how you think of God the Father. He's good and he does the right thing. He loves you in the sense of providing for you. But you think of him as distant or detached. If so, think of his kindness. Let the word play on your imagination. God is kind. He shows us kindness. Substitute it for other words you might use. Instead of saying, "God has answered my prayer," say, "My

Father has been kind to me by answering my prayer". Instead of saying, "Clara was a great help on Saturday," say, "God kindly sent me Clara to help on Saturday". Each day reflect on how God is being kind to you. And think of Jesus as the Father's kindness in person. "But when the kindness and love of God our Saviour appeared," says Paul in Titus 3 v 4-5, "he saved us, not because of righteous things we had done, but because of his mercy". The Father's kindness has "appeared" and it looks like Jesus. If you want to see the kindness of God, then look at the life and death of Jesus. This is the measure of God's kindness. This is divine kindness clothed in human flesh. This is his kindness to you.

Or listen to God speaking through the prophet Jeremiah:

> *They will be my people, and I will be their God ... I will make an everlasting covenant with them:* **I will never stop doing good to them**, *and I will inspire them to fear me, so that they will never turn away from me.* **I will rejoice in doing them good** *and will assuredly plant them in this land with all my heart and soul.*
>
> *(Jeremiah 32 v 38-41)*

Our Father will "never stop doing good" to us (even if life doesn't always feel good). And he doesn't do us good simply because it's in his "job description". He will rejoice to do us good! He does it with "all [his] heart and soul".

One kindness of the Father is that he welcomes us into his presence through prayer. He delights to hear his children talk to him. He rejoices to do us good in response to our prayers.

PRAYING WITH JESUS

Jesus teaches his disciples to pray in the so-called Sermon on the Mount (Matthew 5 – 7). And this teaching on prayer is all about seeing God as our Father. Fifteen times in the sermon Jesus speaks of "your Father" and most of them are clustered around his teaching on prayer.[18] Seeing God as our Father radically changes your attitude to religious duties. It turns religion into *relationship*.

But the most astonishing phrase in Jesus' teaching is not the phrase "your Father", but the phrase "*our* Father", which begins the Lord's Prayer (Matthew 6 v 9). The point is not just that Christians are family together with one another—though that's true. The point is that we pray with Jesus and with Jesus we say, "Our Father". Your Father in heaven is the Father of Jesus. The relationship that *Jesus* has with God the Father is now the same relationship that *you* have with God the Father.

Imagine the scene. The disciples have watched Jesus pray. They've sensed the intimacy he has with God. They can see Jesus has a unique, close relationship with God. They're still piecing together exactly what this means. What they don't yet quite realise is that Jesus is God: eternally sharing one divine being, eternally loved by the Father. For Jesus, the intimacy of heaven is continued here on earth in the intimacy of prayer. And then Jesus walks over to one of them, puts an arm round his shoulder and says, "This ... is how you should pray: 'Our Father.'" In other words: *Pray with me. Share my relationship with God. For you are loved as I am loved.*

John Calvin says, "[Christ], while he is the true Son, has of himself been given us as a brother that what he has of his own by nature may become ours by benefit of adoption."[19]

Let's break that down so we digest it properly. First, Jesus is "the true Son of God". He is the only begotten Son. There has never been another divine Son. From before time, Jesus has been in an intimate relationship of mutual love and delight with God the Father.

Second, Jesus has "been given [to] us". He has been wrapped up in paper, as it were, and given as a gift. He is given to us "as a brother". He took on human flesh to become one with us so we could be one with him. So here we are: tightly bound together by faith. You and Jesus—you can't be separated!

Third, "… that what he has of his own nature…" What is his by nature? He is the eternally begotten. His nature has always been a shared nature with the Father and the Spirit. I know this is hard to get our heads round: Father and Son—sharing one being, bound together in love. Try to think how deep this goes in the identity of Jesus. He is eternally the Son. There was never a time when he was not the Son. Throughout the entire span of human history and throughout the entire span of eternity—which is without span!—the Father and the Son have been in a relationship of deep love and joy.

Fourth—and here's the point—this is what Jesus now gives to us: this relationship, this love, this joy. Jesus is given to us so that what is his by nature, says Calvin, "may become ours by benefit of adoption"! His Father becomes our Father. His experience of paternal love becomes our experience of paternal love. His intimacy and joy become our intimacy and joy. His access to God in prayer becomes our access to God in prayer. On the night he was betrayed, Jesus prayed, "… that they may be brought to complete unity. Then the world will know that you sent me and have loved them even as you have loved me" (John 17 v 23). We are loved with the same love with which God loves Jesus.

DO YOU PAY YOUR TAXES?

There's a rather strange Gospel story in which the collectors of the temple tax ask Peter whether Jesus has paid his tax bill. Jesus says to Peter:

> *"From whom do the kings of the earth collect duty and taxes—from their own children or from others?" "From*

> *others," Peter answered. "Then the children are exempt,"*
> *Jesus said to him.*   *(Matthew 17 v 25-26)*

In other words, Jesus doesn't have to pay a tax for the upkeep of God's house because he is God's Son. He's exempt because he's the child—not of the kings of the earth but of the King of heaven. You might well expect a lodger to contribute to household expenses. But Jesus is the Son, not a tenant. Imagine a father invoicing his four-year-old child for unpaid rent!

But then, to avoid offence, Jesus makes provision for the payment of the tax. He tells Peter to catch a fish in whose mouth Peter will find a four-drachma coin. The story ends with Jesus saying, "Take it and give it to them for my tax and yours" (Matthew 17 v 27). The punchline of the story is those final two words: *"and yours"*. Peter is in the same situation as Jesus! Along with Jesus, Peter will pay the tax to avoid offence. But, along with Jesus, Peter is exempt. Why? Because, along with Jesus, Peter is a son of God. The same is true of you if you're in Christ. You're not a tenant in God's household; you're a child. You have the same rights and privileges as Jesus, the natural Son.

Luke records a fascinating moment in the life of Jesus that gives a remarkable glimpse into the relationships of the Trinity. "At that time," says Luke 10 v 21, "Jesus, full of joy through the Holy Spirit, said, 'I praise you, Father, Lord of heaven and earth, because you have hidden these things from the wise and learned, and revealed them to little children. Yes, Father, for this is what you were pleased to do.'" Jesus experiences joy "through the Holy Spirit". The Holy Spirit is the love through whom the Father and Son delight in one another. And here Jesus rejoices because others are sharing the delight of the triune God.

Not only that: Jesus says this is what the Father was "pleased to do". He uses the past tense—"Yes, Father, for this is what you *were* pleased to do"—because our participation in triune joy is the fulfilment of the Father's eternal plan. This was always the plan and now it's being realised. Adopting us as his children is not merely the Father's duty. It's his pleasure.

PRAYING BY THE SPIRIT

God sent Jesus, the Son by nature, so that you could become a son or daughter by adoption. But God wasn't finished. It's not enough for him to make you his child. He wants you to *feel* like his child and *live* like his child. So God sends the Spirit so we can feel the intimacy and confidence of being his children.

> *For those who are led by the Spirit of God are the children of God. The Spirit you received does not make you slaves, so that you live in fear again; rather, the Spirit you received brought about your adoption to sonship. And by him we cry, "Abba, Father." The Spirit himself testifies with our spirit that we are God's children.*
>
> *(Romans 8 v 14-16)*

If you don't know that you're a child, then you'll live like a slave with a sense of obligation and a fear of rejection. So God the Father sends his Spirit to lead us, just as he led the people of Israel from slavery to freedom through the pillars of cloud and fire (Exodus 13 v 21-22).

Remember the Israelites in the desert: God had rescued them from slavery in Egypt, describing the nation as "my firstborn son" (Exodus 4 v 22-23). But there were times when the Israelites wanted to turn back. They were alone in the desert, surrounded by hostile nations. That's fine if you're a child of the living God because you have every expectation of his provision and protection. But if you don't see yourself as a child, then Egypt seems a better option.

I remember hearing about summer camps for Ukrainian street children. When they first arrived, the children would hide food. Having lived without loving parents, they never knew when their next meal might come. So they hoarded food at every opportunity. They only stopped as they grew confident in the care of the camp leaders. And it's only when you see yourself as a child of God that you stop looking back to slavery and are set free to serve God sacrificially, confident that he will protect and provide.

"Because we are his children," says Paul in Galatians 4 v 6, "God has sent the Spirit of his Son into our hearts, prompting us to call out, '*Abba*, Father'" (NLT). Notice how he describes the Spirit as "the Spirit of his Son". Remember the principle of three and one. The Persons of the Trinity are one being so to encounter the Spirit is to encounter the Son. This means the experience that the Spirit gives us is nothing less than the experience of the Son. Through the Spirit we experience what the Son experiences: the joy and love and confidence of being a child of God the Father.

The early theologian Augustine argues in his book *On the Trinity* that, just as the Son is eternally begotten, so the Spirit is eternally given. He is given by the Father to the Son as the bond of love, the link between the Father and Son. So eternally the Son experiences his sonship through the Spirit. And now the Son gives the Spirit to us so that we can enjoy the same experience of sonship, so that we can enjoy being loved by the Father.

What does this look like? "By [the Spirit] we cry, '*Abba*, Father.'" Because we are his children, God has sent the Spirit of his Son into our hearts, prompting us to call out, "*Abba*, Father" (Romans 8 v 15).

THE JOY OF ADOPTION

My friend and his wife have adopted a son. When what they called "Name Day" arrived—the day when the legal process of adoption was complete—they told their son that he was "Ben Grayson"[20]. Ben went very thoughtful for a moment. Then he looked up and said confidently, "Yes, I am". That wasn't Ben's verdict on the *legal* process—which presumably had somewhat passed him by. That was Ben's verdict on the *relational* process. He said "Yes, I am" because he *feels* loved like a son and because the Graysons *feel* like his parents. That what our spirits are saying when, through the Holy Spirit, we cry "*Abba*, Father".

Without the Spirit of the Son we wouldn't pray. If you don't believe me then try this: right now, wherever you are, ask the President of the United States for a gift. It is, of course, a ridiculous thing to do. He is (probably) not there with you, and even if he were, he would have no reason to respond. Yet Christians routinely do something even more preposterous. We ask the King of heaven to give us gifts with every expectation that he can and will hear us. Why? Because the Spirit of God testifies to our spirits that we are God's children and prompts us to call on God as our Father. We pray because we believe our prayers don't simply hit the ceiling and bounce back down. However distant God may feel in the moment or however perfunctory our praying may be, we pray because we have some sense that God hears us. That is the work of the Spirit. The Spirit connects us to the Father, assuring us that he's our Father and that he delights to hear our cry.

THE SPIRIT'S MIGHTY WORK

Here's the amazing thing: the Spirit's work in our hearts is so mighty that we hardly ever think about it. We pray without a second thought. We take it for granted. There's a sense in which every time we pray we ought to hesitate. "Can I really do this? Can I really approach God? Can I really ask him for things?" That would make sense. After all, we're approaching the one before whom even angels hide their faces. And yet we don't hesitate because the Spirit testifies to our hearts that God is a kind and generous Father who delights to hear our prayer. The irony is that one of the most powerful works of God is so powerful we barely notice it!

The nineteenth-century preacher Charles Spurgeon once said, "It is impossible for you to love God without the strong conclusive evidence that God loves you". He went on to tell the story of a woman who was full of doubts. It turned out she knew she loved Christ, but she was afraid he didn't love her. "Oh," said Spurgeon, "that is a doubt that will never trouble me; never, by any possibility, because I am sure of this, that the heart is so naturally corrupt, that love to God could never get there without God first putting it there." Spurgeon comments:

> *You may rest quite certain, that if you love God, it is a fruit, and not a root. It ... did not get there by the force of any goodness in you. You may conclude, with absolute certainty, that God loves you if you love God. There never was any difficulty on his part. It always was on your part, and now that the difficulty is gone from you there is no more difficulty left. O let our hearts rejoice and be filled with great delight, because the Saviour has loved us and given himself for us.*[21]

How does God the Father relate to us? One answer is that he hears our prayers. Indeed, he delights to hear our prayers and he delights to give good things to his children:

> *Which of you, if your son asks for bread, will give him a stone? Or if he asks for a fish, will give him a snake?*

*If you, then, though you are evil, know how to give good
gifts to your children, how much more will your Father in
heaven give good gifts to those who ask him!*

(*Matthew 7 v 9-11*)

And how do we respond? We pray! Our prayers are never
a burden to our Father. He delights to hear us and he is
honoured by our prayers. Imagine you have a father who
is wealthy, but cares little for you. You won't bother asking
him for anything because you assume he's unwilling to respond. Now imagine you have a father who is generous, but
poor. You won't bother asking him for some things because
you know he's unable to respond—you don't want to em-
barrass him by asking for what he can't provide. But when
we bring our requests before God, we're affirming that he's
both willing and able. We glorify both his power and love.
We're treating him as the kind, capable Father that he is.
And so he's honoured by our prayers.

You may have come across the idea that making childlike requests in prayer is basic spirituality from which we're
invited to move on to contemplative prayer and even to silence. And certainly it's good to spend time meditating on
God's word, character, work and love. It's good to respond
with adoration and worship. But we never graduate from
childlike requests. Childlike requests are *advanced* spirituality.
Placing a child among his disciples, Jesus said, "Whoever
takes the lowly position of this child is the greatest in the
kingdom of heaven" (Matthew 18 v 4). There's nothing
greater than coming as a child before God the Father.

We mustn't think of prayer as a task we need to perform. It's a way of relating to a person and enjoying our
relationship with them. God is a loving Father who delights to hear us, and prayer is our opportunity to spend
time with him. Personally I find it helpful to think of

prayer as a place to be with God. Christ has ascended into heaven and we're in Christ, so in Christ we ascend to heaven (Hebrews 10 v 19-22). So I imagine myself stepping into heaven to be with God. Or, because it's hard to conceive of heaven, I think of God filling the space in which I'm located. Heaven seeps into my world. I create this space in my imagination: on the outside is the rest of the world; inside I'm with my heavenly Father.

Close your eyes. Imagine God the Father in the room with you, surrounding you with his love. If you're in a noisy place, then start by focusing on that noise. Then let the noise become muffled in the background, replaced by a sense of God's love. And then just talk—out loud if you can or in your head if other people are around.

Don't worry if your imagination doesn't work like this. The key thing is to think of prayer as relating to your Father rather than performing a task. Think of God as your Father and then just talk. Just talk to God about what's on your mind. Or start with him: think about who he is and all he's done for you. And then respond with grateful praise. If you're not sure where to begin, begin with the Lord's Prayer (see Matthew 6 v 9-13). Fill out each line of the Lord's Prayer with your own praise and requests.

PUTTING IT INTO PRACTICE

We pray to a Father who loves to hear us. So throughout this coming week, start all your prayers with the words, "My Father". Or, if you're praying with other people, "Our Father". Some of you start your prayers with some variation of "God" or "Lord". There's nothing wrong with that. But try this: with your words and with your heart begin, "My Father". If you do this already, then try to pause as you say the word "Father" so you truly relish being a child of God.

ACTION
Each time you pray this week, start by saying "My Father" or "Our Father".

MIKE AND EMMA'S MONDAY MORNING
Ten minutes later Emma takes a bite of toast and opens her Bible. She reads a few verses and then she closes her eyes to pray. "Father, may Mike have a good day at work. Please bless…" Jamie bursts into the room. "Where's my school sweater?" Sam's not far behind. "Have you seen my homework?" And Poppy… Where's Poppy?

"Sam, you look for Jamie's sweater. Jamie, you look for Sam's homework. I'll look for Poppy." Another time of prayer disrupted. But Emma carries on praying as she climbs the stairs. "Thank you, Father, that you're always there, always ready to listen, even when my prayers are a bit of a jumble."

REFLECTION QUESTIONS
- The previous chapter ended with a challenge to thank God for sending difficult things to make you more like Jesus. How have you got on?
- How do you think of God the Father? Do you think of him as kind?
- Look at the Lord's Prayer—the prayer Jesus teaches us in the Sermon on the Mount (Matthew 6 v 9-13). What difference does it make to see each line as a request from a child to their Father?
- List the reasons why someone might hesitate to pray to God.
- List the reasons why, wonderfully, we don't need to hesitate to pray.

IN EVERY FAILURE
WE CAN ENJOY
THE SON'S GRACE

There's a series of the British TV comedy *Blackadder* which is set in the First World War. One of the central characters is the aristocratic General Melchett, played by Stephen Fry. General Melchett sends his troops to their death from the safety of his office without a care. At one point he says to Private Baldrick, "Don't worry, my boy. If you should falter, remember that Captain Darling and I are behind you." To which Blackadder sarcastically adds, "About 35 miles behind you".

AHEAD, NOT BEHIND

Jesus is not behind us; he's ahead of us. Hebrews 12 v 2-3 says:

> [*Let us fix*] *our eyes on Jesus, the pioneer and perfecter of faith. For the joy that was set before him he endured the cross, scorning its shame, and sat down at the right hand of the throne of God. Consider him who endured such opposition from sinners, so that you will not grow weary and lose heart.*

The word "pioneer" means "the champion, the example, the One who leads the way".²² We're to follow our King into battle. He leads the way and we follow. For Christ it meant death. And we enter the battle with that same willingness to die—certainly to die to self. Jesus asks *everything of us*, but he asks *nothing of us* that he himself has not first endured. Unlike General Melchett, Jesus is not a general behind the lines.

In the final movie of the *Lord of the Rings* trilogy, the city of Gondor has been temporarily defended. But now the enemy armies of Mordor are massing for a further assault on the world of men. The situation looks hopeless. Nevertheless, Aragorn, the true king, decides to take the battle to the enemy in the hope that maybe he can buy time for Frodo and Sam, who are trying to destroy the ring, the secret of the enemy's power. As Aragorn marches out to meet the enemy, the gates of Mordor open and its evil army spews out of the Black Gate. Aragorn and his men are vastly outnumbered. At one point a stillness falls across the battlefield. And then Aragorn raises his sword and charges into battle. For a moment he is alone. And then Pippin and Merry, the young hobbits, follow after him. His example has inspired them to take courage and enter the fray. Soon the hobbits are followed by the rest of the forces of Gondor.

Jesus is our Champion, our Commander, our Captain. He promised, "I will build my church" (Matthew 16 v 18). He took on Satan, sin and death, and rose victorious.

But Jesus is not only ahead of us. He's also over us. "God placed all things under [Christ's] feet and appointed him to be head over everything for the church," says Paul in Ephesians 1 v 22. It's no surprise to hear that Jesus has been given all authority. But notice *why* he has been placed over everything: "for the church". Think about that for a moment. God placed Jesus over all things for us—for you. Jesus rules from heaven "for the church". He protects his people and guides our mission. He sends the Holy Spirit to equip us for service (Ephesians 4 v 7-16).

We don't have to co-ordinate the forces of global mission. We don't have to work out the most strategic thing to do. Christ builds his church and organises his people. Our job is to offer him our lives, to be faithful witnesses, to serve him. And then let him use us as he chooses in his grand strategy to build his church.

Jesus is actively involved in the life and mission of his people now—right now. It's all too easy to think that his work took place a long time ago and that he himself is a long way away. This was how I used to think of Jesus. But this sense that Jesus is distant is wrong—very wrong.

Just consider how involved he is throughout the book of Acts. Again and again Jesus intervenes from heaven.[23] He appears in order to comfort Stephen as Stephen faces martyrdom in Acts 7. He appears to Paul on the road to Damascus to call him to faith and set the agenda for his life work in Acts 9. He speaks from heaven to Peter to challenge him to take the gospel across cultural boundaries in Acts 10 – 11. In Acts 9 v 34 Peter tells a bedridden man, "Jesus Christ heals you". Feel the weight of that statement. Jesus may not be physically present on earth. But he's still very much involved. He's spiritually present—that is, present by his Spirit. And that means he is powerfully active.

What's Jesus doing now? He's healing, speaking, saving, comforting, building and equipping.

BUSY DOING NOTHING

But there's another answer to that question and it's the answer that must come first. What's Jesus doing now? *Nothing.* It's a more profound answer than it might at first appear to be! In fact it's an answer with the power to bring comfort whenever we fail.

Consider how the writer of Hebrews describes Jesus and ask yourself, "What is Jesus doing now?"

> *[11] Day after day every priest stands and performs his religious duties; again and again he offers the same sacrifices, which can never take away sins. [12] But when this priest had offered for all time one sacrifice for sins, he sat down at the right hand of God, [13] and since that time he waits for his enemies to be made his footstool. [14] For by one sacrifice he has made perfect for ever those who are being made holy.* (Hebrews 10 v 11-14)

What is Jesus doing now? Answer: sitting (v 12) and waiting (v 13). Many of our songs speak of Jesus standing (and there are three occasions in the New Testament where Jesus is said to stand). But most of the time the New Testament talks of him sitting. The point is this: he sits because his work of salvation is done. "It is finished," he cried on the cross (John 19 v 30). He has made complete atonement for our sin. There's nothing left for him to do.

Yet for Jesus, doing nothing is a full-time job! He is, as the old song says, "busy doing nothing". Jesus is our representative. What's he doing? He is representing us in heaven. He's in heaven on our behalf.

When you become a Christian, you're united with Christ by faith through the Spirit. That means that his death was your death and his resurrection is your life. But our union with Christ doesn't just mean his *past* actions were done on our behalf. We're united with Christ *now* in heaven. "God raised us up with Christ," says Paul, "and seated us with him in the heavenly realms in Christ Jesus" (Ephesians 2 v 6). He represents us before the Father. By faith we're with him in heaven. His rest is our rest. His place in heaven is our place in heaven. He's our guarantee and our security.

Jesus is our High Priest, and the sacrifice that he offered was himself. And his sacrifice was complete and sufficient. "Unlike the other high priests," says Hebrews 7 v 27, "he does not need to offer sacrifices day after day". His sacrifice was "once for all when he offered himself". There was another big limitation faced by previous priests: sooner or later they all died. "Death prevented them from continuing in office" (v 23). But not Jesus. "Because Jesus lives for ever, he has a permanent priesthood" (v 24). Jesus has the job for life and his life is eternal.

Add it all together and what do you get? "Therefore [Jesus] is able to save completely those who come to God through him, because he always lives to intercede for them" (v 25). When you think of Jesus, your first thought should be to think of him before the Father on your behalf.

So he's always busy doing his job—and his job is to do nothing. He intercedes for us, not through some action he must perform in heaven but by his very presence. He himself is the living sign and pledge of our salvation. His right to come before God is your right to come before God. His location is your location. As long as Jesus is in heaven, our place there is guaranteed. As long as Jesus has the Father's approval, we have the Father's approval. As long as Jesus lives, our life is guaranteed. And Jesus lives for ever!

When Peter and John were hauled in front of the Jewish leaders to account for their "crime" of healing a crippled man, Peter said:

> *It is by the name of Jesus Christ of Nazareth, whom you crucified but whom God raised from the dead, that this man stands before you healed ... Salvation is found in no one else, for there is no other name under heaven given to mankind by which we must be saved.*
>
> *(Acts 4 v 10, 12)*

The "name" of Jesus represents his character and work. His work on the cross may be finished. But its implications live on. It's the basis by which God heals and saves. God is active in the world in the name of Jesus. And he's active in your life in the name of Jesus. God forgives your sin through the death of Christ. In every failure we can enjoy the grace that comes to us through Jesus.

The last lines of Augustus Toplady's hymn "A debtor to mercy alone" are "More happy but not more secure, the glorified spirits in heaven". The "glorified spirits" are Christians who've already died and are now in the presence of God. They're "more happy" because their earthly sufferings are over. And they're completely secure because they're in God's presence, far from any threat or temptation. But Christians on earth are *just as secure* as those in heaven because *Jesus* is in heaven on our behalf. Only if Jesus were to be thrown out of heaven would our place in heaven be in jeopardy. And that's never going to happen!

Pause for a moment to think what this means for you. Every failure, every sin, every dark thought might seem to throw our future into doubt. Am I really accepted by God? Can I really be forgiven? Can I still call heaven my home? Lift the eyes of faith to see Jesus in the presence of God on your behalf.

Because we've failed to live in obedience to God, we deserve eternal punishment. Feel the weight of that. Look into the infinite darkness of judgment. And then lift your eyes to see Christ: your Christ, your sacrifice. Light, love and joy flood into view. This is how we enjoy Christ. We bring our failure to him and receive his grace.

LETTING GO OF GUILT

How do we respond? How do we relate to Jesus, our Man in heaven?

We do what he does: we need to get busy doing nothing! Of course there's lots we should be doing as Christians. Jesus is at work, as we've already seen, ensuring the message of salvation goes to those for whom he died. And we share in that work.

But when it comes to earning our salvation or winning the Father's approval or impressing other people, we need to be busy doing nothing. There is nothing to do. What do I need to put right my sins and my failures? Nothing. It is finished.

But we kind of need to be *busy doing nothing* because we so easily start trying to do something. We actively need to stop ourselves trying to prove ourselves. We default to trying to win God's approval through our actions—and we need to stop. If you're doing things to impress God or to impress other people, then stop. Rest. Relax. Enjoy God's grace. Rest in the finished work of Christ. Hear him cry, "It is finished".

Let's ask John Owen to help us again.[24] Owen urges Christians to "lay down their sins at the cross of Christ, upon his shoulders". He speaks of this as faith's "great and bold venture". Imagine someone comes to you with an investment opportunity: "Stake everything you have on me, and I'll give you outstanding returns". That's the venture to which Jesus calls us. There's no money involved. There's nothing we could give to earn our stake in Christ. But we are invited to stake ourselves "on the grace, faithfulness and truth of God". At times it will feel like a risk. After all, our sins can loom so large. Is the death of one man really up to the task? The pleasures of this world are enticing. Is the future Jesus promises worth it? Yes, Jesus is a safe investment every time. So Owen invites us to stand by the cross and say:

Ah! Jesus is bruised for my sins, and wounded for my transgressions, and the chastisement of my peace is upon him. He is thus made sin for me. Here I give up my sins

*to him that is able to bear them. He requires me to open
my hands, release my grip and let him deal with my sin.
And that I heartily consent to.*[25]

You might think this is what happens when someone first
becomes a Christian. And, of course, you're right. But
Owen adds, "This is *every day's work*; I know not how any
peace can be maintained with God without it."[26] Every day
we need to stop trying to make things right with God. We
need to let go of our sin and hand it to Jesus. We need to be
busy doing nothing.

Think of your sin. The sins you've committed today. The
sins it feels as though you commit every day. Then imagine handing them to Jesus one by one. Open your hands.
Release your grip. Say with Owen, "Here I give up my sins
to him that is able to bear them". Feel the weight lift from
your heart. Feel your shoulders relax. Jesus has taken your
burden and borne it at the cross in your place.

*My sin, oh, the bliss of this glorious thought!
My sin, not in part but the whole,
Is nailed to the cross, and I bear it no more,
Praise the Lord, praise the Lord, O my soul!*[27]

This is what it means to enjoy a relationship with Jesus.

Or think of it like this. Every day Jesus says to us in the
gospel message, *I'll do you a deal. I'll take your failures, sin, guilt,
bitterness, curse, wrath and death, and in return I'll give you joy, love,
life, righteousness and peace.* Owen calls it "blessed bartering".[28]
Our job is gladly to accept the deal, hand over our sin and
receive Christ's love.

"What?" asks Owen. "Shall we daily come to him with our
filth, our guilt, our sins?" Is this really what Jesus wants—to have
our mess given to him day after day? This is Owen's answer:
"There is not any thing that Jesus Christ is more delighted with

than that his saints should always have communion with him in this business of giving and receiving."[29]

FIXING OUR EYES ON JESUS

We began this chapter with the exhortation of Hebrews 12 v 2 to "[fix] our eyes on Jesus". Jesus is the image of God, the word of God, the glory of God. To see Jesus is to see the Father. Jesus reflects the Father's glory. The light of God's glory is perfectly reflected in the image or mirror of his Son. The Father sees in his Son a perfect reflection of his perfections. And so in this way the Son shares the Father's glory. From all eternity God's perfections pour out from the Father to the Son and back to the Father through the Spirit. So our primary response is to *look* to Christ and to *worship* Christ. For we see "the light of the knowledge of God's glory displayed in the face of Christ" (2 Corinthians 4 v 6). We delight in his perfect character. We revel in his finished work. We rest on what he has already done through his life, cross and resurrection.

And we respond to Jesus by following him through faith into heaven:

> *Therefore, since we have a great high priest who has*
> *ascended into heaven, Jesus the Son of God, let us hold*
> *firmly to the faith we profess ... Let us then approach*
> *God's throne of grace with confidence, so that we may*
> *receive mercy and find grace to help us in our time of need.*
> *(Hebrews 4 v 14, 16)*

How does Christ relate to us now? He sits in heaven on our behalf. He's our guarantee of a place with God. His work on the cross is complete. But it goes on speaking. It speaks to the Father as a permanent sign that the price of sin has been paid in full. And it speaks to us with a message of comfort when we're besieged by doubt.

We respond by seeing Jesus in heaven on our behalf. We give up our attempts to remove our guilt, establish our identity or prove ourselves. Instead we rest on his finished work. We follow Jesus by faith and come before God's throne with confidence.

And we respond with love. When we look at Jesus, seated at the Father's side, we see the Friend who laid down his life for his friends (John 15 v 12-13). We see the Husband who gave himself up for his bride (Ephesians 5 v 25). We see the Good Shepherd who laid down his life for his sheep (John 10 v 11).

You can't conjure love out of thin air. You can't love someone simply as an act of will or in response to a command. Not really. But you can fix your eyes on Jesus. You can look back to his work on the cross; you can look up to his presence in heaven for you; and you can look forward to the day when he returns for his people. "We love because he first loved us" (1 John 4 v 19).

And there's nothing more godly or godlike than loving Jesus. The only object of the Father's love in eternity is the eternal Son, loved through the Spirit. And the primary object of the Father's love in history is the Son made human. So when we love the Son, we do so alongside the Father.[30]

PUTTING IT INTO PRACTICE

Have a go at Owen's "blessed bartering". Think back over the past day or week. Make a mental list of all the things you have left undone that you ought to have done, and the things you have done that you ought not to have done. Think of your sins of thought, word and deed. And then hand them over to Jesus. Imagine them nailed to an empty cross. Stand by the cross and say, "Jesus was wounded for my sins". And then receive from him love, life, righteousness and peace.

ACTION
Every day this week find time to identify what you have done to impress others. Then hear the words, "It is finished".

MIKE AND EMMA'S MONDAY MORNING
Mike closes his eyes again and heads off in his imagination to a place far away from this crowded carriage. He's just about to dive into the blue water of a tropical lagoon when someone spills tea down his shirt. He swears. Immediately he flushes. And not just because warm tea is spreading across his stomach. He's embarrassed. "I'm so sorry. Really sorry. It's the delay, the standing. I'm not normally so grumpy." The young woman holding what remains of her tea is just as embarrassed. "No, no, it's my fault," she says as she squeezes past and disappears.

He had sworn. Out loud. "Where did that come from?" he asks himself. But immediately he knows the answer. "From my proud, selfish heart." He thinks about yesterday's sermon. "There's nothing worthy in me," he thinks, "but Christ is more than worthy". He thinks of Christ seated at God's side. "Christ has sorted everything," he says. Out loud. A few heads turn in confusion. Mike fakes a cough. And then smiles to himself. Christ is in heaven on his behalf.

REFLECTION QUESTIONS
- The previous chapter ended with a challenge to start each prayer with "My Father" or "Our Father". How have you got on? What difference has it made?
- What do you find challenging about the Christian life? In what ways has Jesus already done what he asks of you?
- List all the things you do to earn God's approval or impress other people… And then cross them all out and write across the page "It is finished!"

- How will we live if we think we need to earn God's approval? How will we live if we are confident we have God's approval in Christ?
- When are you over-busy? What's the fear that drives your busyness? How might Christ seated in heaven or ruling from heaven calm your flustered heart?

IN EVERY PAIN
WE CAN ENJOY
THE SON'S PRESENCE

A few years ago our church sent someone to serve Christ in Asia. Let's call him Tom. So suppose you came to me and said, "What's Tom like?" I would say, "He's great. He has a strong devotion to Christ. He's diligent, disciplined, sacrificial. He's good with people. A good guy." To which you might say, "Hang on a moment. Tom's not here. He's in central Asia. You haven't seen him for two years. How can you know what he's like?" I would reply, "Of course I know Tom. I've spent time with him. We ate meals together. We hung out together. We served together. I saw him in action and heard him talk. I know what Tom's like because I know what he was like when he was living here."

The same is true of Jesus. How can we know what Jesus is like now? After all, he's not here on earth any more. We can't see him or touch him or hear him speak. How can we trust him? The answer is: we know what Jesus is like now because we know what he was like when he was living here on earth.

Of course, people change. Perhaps Tom is not the man he used to be. But with Jesus it's *always* true. His character never changes. The Bible says that "Jesus Christ is the same yesterday and today and for ever" (Hebrews 13 v 8). With Jesus, past behaviour is a completely reliable indicator of his attitude towards us now.

So, as we read the Gospel stories, we discover not only what Jesus was like but also what he is like now. We discover not only how he related to his people *then* but also how he relates to his people *now*.

In this chapter I want to encourage you to read the Gospels with this thought in mind. Keep asking yourself, "What do this story, these words, this miracle show me about Jesus and the way he relates to people like me?" Let's have a quick taster.

TO THOSE WHO FEEL LOSS, JESUS SAYS, "DON'T CRY" (LUKE 7 v 11-17)

I wonder if you sometimes think Jesus sits in heaven looking down on your life much as you watch the television. Getting bored? Where's the remote? Change the channel. Or maybe you think of him like one of those security guards who sit in front of a bank of screens, looking at all of them without ever really being interested in any of them. Maybe you imagine Jesus with a bank of screens showing the lives of all his people, and occasionally he glances at your screen without much interest. An account from Luke 7 will help us think this through:

In the town of Nain, Jesus sees a funeral procession. The only son of a widow has died. Here is a woman facing deep emotional loss. But her life has also just become precarious. In a culture in which only men earn income, she has already lost her husband and now she has lost her son. "When the Lord saw her," Luke 7 v 13 says, "his heart went out to her and he said, 'Don't cry.'" Think about that phrase for a moment: "his heart went out to her". Luke could have left it out or simply said, "Jesus chose to help her". But instead he highlights the compassion of Jesus.

The Jesus who saw the widow in Nain is the same Jesus who sees your distress. His heart goes out to you just as it did to the widow. And Jesus says to you through his word and by his Spirit, "Don't cry".

It's not a rebuke. It's not that crying is wrong. On another occasion Jesus himself cries with a bereaved woman (John 11 v 35). No, this is a word of comfort. *Don't cry. There is hope.*

The story ends: "The dead man sat up and began to talk, and Jesus gave him back to his mother" (Luke 7 v 15). Jesus raises him from the dead, but it's not just a story about someone coming back to life. It's about a son being restored to his mother—a story of loss and restoration. "Jesus gave him back to his mother." Everything will be all right. Maybe not today; maybe not tomorrow. But a day of restoration is coming.

Jesus is not up in heaven uninterested in your life. He didn't abandon us. He's the same person he was 2,000 years ago. Imagine the moment when Jesus sees this widow. Imagine the look on his face. That is how he looks when he sees your distress. And he says, "Don't cry".

TO THOSE WHO FEEL SHAME, JESUS SAYS, "GO IN PEACE" (LUKE 7 v 36-50 AND 8 v 42-48)

Luke tells the stories of two women. The first invites herself to a party to anoint Jesus' feet; the second pushes through a crowd to touch Jesus. Jesus says exactly the same words to both women (though depending on which Bible version you use, your English translation might hide this): "Your faith has saved you; go in peace" (Luke 7 v 50; 8 v 48).

The first woman receives forgiveness for her public sins. She's notorious. She's described as "a woman in that town who lived a sinful life" (Luke 7 v 37). This is what makes her actions so remarkable. She exposes herself to public condemnation to wash the feet of Jesus. She's laying it all on the line. She has every reason to think she might be mocked, abused or even violently removed. She's lived a life of shame and now she risks still more shame. The woman comes in turmoil and Jesus says, "Go in peace". She comes in shame and Jesus says, "Your sins are forgiven" (v 48).

The second woman received healing for her hidden sickness. But this was no ordinary sickness. Under the Law of Moses, in common with many other conditions, women who were menstruating were unclean (Leviticus 15 v 19-31). This law was designed as a picture of sin. If you touched them, you became unclean. But this woman had some kind of haemorrhaging that meant she was *continually* bleeding as if she had a permanent period. So if *at any point* someone touched her, they would become unclean. Thankfully, this law of uncleanness no longer applies, but imagine living like that. Imagine the shame.

This is why she was so afraid when Jesus demanded to know who'd touched him. By touching his cloak, she would have made Jesus unclean. Her actions would be seen as rude and intrusive—almost aggressive. But instead of being offended, Jesus says, "Daughter, your faith has healed you. Go in peace." Instead of uncleanness flowing from the woman to Jesus, cleansing has flowed from Jesus to her.

There may be turmoil in your heart. You may carry a deep sense of guilt. Perhaps you struggle to sleep as a result. Perhaps you harm yourself. Perhaps there's something you turn over in your head again and again. It's said that the author Mark Twain (though it might have been Arthur Conan Doyle) once sent a dozen friends a telegram saying, "Flee at once—all is discovered". They all left town immediately. Imagine you received that message: "Flee at once—all is discovered."

What would come to mind? You may be struggling with an eating disorder. You may look at porn. You may have a criminal conviction no one in the church knows about. Or it might be how much you spend on shoes, or that last week you ate a whole tub of ice cream in one sitting. What's your secret? What's your shame? If you trust Jesus, then he says to you, "Your sins are forgiven ... Go in peace".

TO THOSE WHO FEEL ANXIOUS, JESUS SAYS, "DON'T BE AFRAID" (LUKE 8 v 40-56)

Think for a moment about something that makes you afraid. What's the worst that could happen? What's your nightmare scenario? I share the fears of Jairus. Jairus' daughter is perilously ill, so he asks Jesus to come to his house before it's too late. Many of my fears centre on my daughters. I never used to be afraid of heights until I became a father. But as soon as I had children, I started imagining them plunging off footpaths. I felt much more vulnerable through my children.

As Jesus is on his way to Jairus' daughter, he is interrupted by the sick woman. You can imagine Jairus hopping from foot to foot while Jesus talks with her. His daughter is dying. Jesus is his last and only hope. His great fear is that Jesus will not get there in time. And then it's too late: Jairus' nightmare scenario arrives. "While Jesus was still speaking, someone came from the house of Jairus, the synagogue leader. 'Your daughter is dead,' he said. 'Don't bother the teacher anymore.' Hearing this, Jesus said to Jairus, 'Don't be afraid; just believe, and she will be healed'" (v 49-50). "Don't be afraid." There's almost a sense in which Jairus is beyond fear. What is there to fear now? The worst has already happened. Yet Jesus says, "Don't be afraid, just believe".

When Jesus reaches the home of Jairus, he says, "She is not dead but asleep" (v 52). Jesus can wake the dead as easily as you and I might wake someone from sleep. For many of us, I suspect, death is our nightmare scenario. Push back beyond our immediate fears and what we fear is death. Whether it's heights or the dark, the lurking fear behind them all is death.

But with Jesus, death is no longer something to be feared. Death is not the end. Jesus offers life after death: eternal life. The worst that can happen has become the gateway to life. Bad things still happen—sometimes very bad things. But we don't need to be afraid. Jesus says to us today in the midst of our fears, "Don't be afraid; just believe".

Luke sets up these stories as signs of the new world that Jesus will create through his death and resurrection. In 8 v 48 Jesus says, "Daughter, your faith has healed you". The word is actually "saved". And in 8 v 50 Jesus literally says, "Don't be afraid; just believe, and she will be *saved*". Luke is a doctor. He knows plenty of words to describe people getting well. But he uses the word "salvation". He wants us to see in these stories a picture of the salvation Jesus offers. A day is coming when "'he will wipe every tear from their eyes. There will be no more death' or mourning or crying or pain, for the old order of things has passed away" (Revelation 21 v 4). In the meantime, Jesus says to you, *Don't cry. Go in peace. Don't be afraid.*

JESUS SYMPATHISES

The One who reigns in heaven is the One who became human. Jesus sympathises with us because he came to earth and took a human body. And he sympathises with us because, when he returned to heaven, he kept a human body. Jesus in heaven has a human body.

> *Therefore, since we have a great high priest who has*
> *ascended into heaven, Jesus the Son of God, let us hold*

firmly to the faith we profess. For we do not have a high
priest who is unable to feel sympathy for our weaknesses,
but we have one who has been tempted in every way, just as
we are—yet he did not sin.   *(Hebrews 4 v 14-15)*

This reference to the sympathy of Jesus is expanded in Hebrews 5. In the Old Testament the high priest was selected
from among the people so that he was able "to deal gently
with those who are ignorant and are going astray, since he
himself is subject to weakness" (Hebrews 5 v 2). It is the
same with Jesus our great high priest.

During the days of Jesus' life on earth, he offered up
prayers and petitions with fervent cries and tears to the one
who could save him from death, and he was heard because
of his reverent submission. Son though he was, he learned
obedience from what he suffered and, once made perfect, he
became the source of eternal salvation for all who
obey him.   *(Hebrews 5 v 7-9)*

In other words, to be fully equipped as a priest who could
sympathise with our weaknesses, Jesus had to become
human, to become weak, to suffer like us. How does Jesus
relate to us? He sympathises with us in our weakness and he
sympathises with us in our temptations.

Commenting on Hebrews 4 v 15, the seventeenth-cen-
tury Puritan Thomas Goodwin says that Christ may have
ascended to the joys of heaven, but "he retains one tender
part and bare place in his heart still unarmed, as it were,
even to suffer with you".[31] In other words, by retaining his
human nature, Christ has chosen to leave himself vulnerable to feeling our pain. As I write, the world beyond my
window is covered in snow. This morning I walked through
the falling snow with hat, scarf and gloves to protect me

from the cold. Imagine I had left one hand exposed so I could experience the full sensation of winter. God as God cannot suffer. Yet God in Christ has retained his humanity so that he still experiences the full sensation of humanity, including human suffering.

"God is love," says Goodwin, "and Christ is love covered over with flesh, yes, our flesh."[32] Christ's experience of life on earth makes possible "a new way of being merciful" because it enables God to feel what we feel.[33] The mercies of God have become human mercies in Christ, with a natural affinity to our struggles.

Let's do an experiment, suggests Goodwin. Think about how becoming a Christian has changed you—your new concern for your spiritual life and your new compassion towards others. That's the work of the Spirit in your heart. Goodwin then asks, does the Spirit have less impact on Jesus? No. "The same Spirit dwells in Christ's heart in heaven that does in yours here," and "that Spirit stirs up in him feelings of mercy infinitely larger towards you than you can have towards yourselves."[34] Your Spirit-empowered compassion is an echo of Christ's Spirit-empowered compassion.

You might wonder whether Christ feels less sympathy now that he's glorified in heaven. Quite the opposite, argues Goodwin. It's true that his knowledge and power are enlarged by his glorification. But his increased knowledge means that he sees all the suffering of his people, and his increased power means his sympathy is not diminished by weariness. "His human affections of love and pity are enlarged in solidity, strength, and reality."[35]

Human beings have a tendency to suffer from "compassion fatigue". The more stories of suffering we see, the less impact they have. We grow immune to their emotional pull. I sometimes feel that if I made an effort to feel empathy with every situation, I would collapse under the weight of pain. But the heart of Jesus is *enlarged* by his glory and power. He can cope with the emotional strain. He feels the suffering of all his people without needing to limit his empathy.

What about when we sin? Surely that makes Christ look away in disgust? Not at all, says Goodwin. "Your very sins move him to pity more than to anger ... Christ takes your side."[36] Parents feel intense compassion when their children are ill. I remember a father once expressing to me the visceral hatred he felt towards the cancer destroying his daughter's body. That's how Christ feels about the sin in our lives. The greater the misery we see, the more pity we feel. And "of all miseries," says Goodwin, "sin is the greatest". So Christ has great compassion on us even when we sin. "You don't know by sinning what blows you give the heart of Christ."[37]

Let me summarise with these words from Goodwin:

> *We can be certain that love which Christ, when on earth, expressed to be in his heart, and which made him die for sinners at the command of his Father, continues in his heart still, now he is in heaven. And it is as quick and as tender as ever it was on earth, even as when he was on the cross.*[38]

The spit of the soldiers on his face, the bite of the whip into his flesh, the pull of the nails on his wrists, the darkened skies that hid his Father's smile—Jesus accepted them all because of his love for you. He could have called on legions of angels to rescue him from the cross, but his love prevented him. That's the love he feels for you today. Now. As you read these words. His love—his love for you—is the same yesterday, today and for ever.

PUTTING IT INTO PRACTICE

How do we experience Christ? We remember Jesus still has a human body and he stills remembers what life on earth is like. Jesus knows what it's like to be you. The only difference is now he has the capacity to sympathise with all of his people.

On its own, Christ's sympathy doesn't change the circumstances you face. But it does mean you don't have to face them alone. It means Jesus is for you in your struggles, even in your struggles with temptation. He doesn't look on with disapproval, waiting for you to mess up. He looks on you with sympathy. He knows what it's like. He understands. He's for you.

The Puritan William Bridge wrote:

> Be sure that you think of Christ in a right way and manner as he suits your condition and as he is held forth in the gospel ... The Scriptures hold forth the person of Christ in ways that make him very amiable to poor sinners:
>
> - Are you accused by Satan, the world or your own conscience? He is called your Advocate.
> - Are you ignorant? He is called the Prophet.
> - Are you guilty of sin? He is called a Priest and High Priest.
> - Are you afflicted with many enemies, inward and outward? He is called a King, and King of kings.
> - Are you in dire straits? He is called your Way.
> - Are you hungry or thirsty? He is called the Bread and Water of Life.
> - Are you afraid you shall fall away and be condemned at the last? He is our second Adam, our representative, in whose death we died and who has satisfied all that God requires of us.

Just as there is no temptation or affliction, but some
promise or other is especially suited to it, so there is no
condition, but some name, some title, some attribute of
Christ is especially suited to it.[39]

Think of a challenge you face or a lack you feel. Then identify some name, some title, some attribute of Christ that is especially suited to it or a story from the Gospels that exemplifies his attitude towards people in your plight.

ACTION
Whenever you struggle this week, think of Jesus looking on with sympathy (rather than disapproval).

MIKE AND EMMA'S MONDAY MORNING
Back at home Emma is ushering the children out of the door. One, two, three. She thinks of Rosie. Four. Every day she thinks of Rosie, their fourth child, born with a malformed heart and dead at three months. Absent and yet always present. Two years on Emma still feels the loss. It hurts. Here on the doorstep it hurts. "Time will heal," people had said. She knows they're trying to be positive. But she doesn't want to "be positive". Sometimes she just wants to weep.

Emma thinks of Jesus weeping with Mary when Lazarus had died. "He didn't give Mary a lecture. He just wept with her. Jesus knew what it was like. After all, Lazarus had been his friend." Emma thinks of the friends who've wept with her. It had been a comfort. But people had stopped talking about it. No one really knows the pain she still feels. "No one?" Her thoughts go back to Jesus. She's been talking as if Jesus belonged in the past. She thinks about Jesus in heaven, looking down into her home. Does Jesus see her broken heart? Yes, surely he does. Does he sympathise with Emma as he did with Mary? Jesus had said, "Surely I am with you always". "I'm not alone," Emma tells herself, "not even in the grief that no one else sees".

REFLECTION QUESTIONS

- The previous chapter ended with a challenge to identify what you've done to impress others and then hear the words, "It is finished". How have you got on?
- Imagine Jesus looking at you from heaven. What expression do you think is on his face?
- Consider three stories from the Gospels. In each case, ask yourself, "What does this story, these words, this miracle show me about Jesus and the way he relates to people like me?"
- When do you feel loss, anxiety or shame? What difference would it make to hear Jesus say, "Don't cry; go in peace; don't be afraid"?
- What aspect of Christ's character or work particularly matches your current concerns?

IN EVERY SUPPER
WE CAN ENJOY
THE SON'S TOUCH

R ecently my friend Tyler—who's six years old—described our church as "Josh's church". Josh is the man who opens up each Sunday morning so he's always there when Tyler arrives. Tyler's parents corrected him: "It's not Josh's church; it's Jesus' church". Tyler looked bemused and then said, "If it's Jesus' church, why does he never come?"

I think that's a charming six-year-old version of an issue we all feel: Jesus is notable by his absence, at least his physical absence. We talk a lot about finding joy in Christ. We overcome temptation, we tell one another, by finding joy in Christ. But how do I enjoy something or someone I can't see or hear or touch?

ANOTHER ADVOCATE

"Anyone who has seen me has seen the Father," said Jesus (John 14 v 9). "That was all well and good for the first disciples," you might say. "But what about me? I haven't seen Jesus. Reading the stories of his encounters with people is all very interesting—attractive even. But it was all such a long time ago. How can I have an encounter with Jesus?"

Answer: another advocate. "I will ask the Father," Jesus told his disciples, "and he will give you another advocate to help you and be with you for ever—the Spirit of truth" (John 14 v 16-17). The word "advocate" is a big word in Greek. It embraces the ideas of an advocate, a strengthener, a witness and a helper. Our advocate is the lawyer by our side, presenting our case, and the witness testifying to the truth about Jesus. Or you might think of a friend speaking up for you when you're criticised, or speaking to you when you're discouraged. Or imagine you've had a really bad day. It's time for a comforting cup of tea. But then you drop the milk on the floor. It feels like the last straw. Your helper says, "You sit down while I clean up and make that cup of tea". This is the Spirit whom Jesus has sent to us.

Notice Jesus calls him *"another* advocate". Jesus is the *first* advocate, and the Spirit replaces him now that Jesus has ascended to heaven. So perhaps the best way to think of how the Spirit is our advocate is to think of how Jesus was an advocate.

On one occasion the religious leaders challenged the disciples: *Why don't you fast like we do?* (Mark 2 v 18-22). Imagine you're a disciple in that moment. You're a fisherman. You don't know much theology. You've perhaps never really thought about fasting. And now the professionals are demanding answers. You haven't got a clue. And these are important people. You could be in big trouble. What do you do? I suspect you look round to see if you can spot Jesus. And when you see him, you immediately feel relieved. He'll know what to say. He'll be your advocate.

On another occasion the disciples are in a boat when a storm blows up (Mark 4 v 35-41). The waves crash over the decks. Drowning is a real possibility. Imagine you're one of the disciples. What do you do? Even the fishermen are frightened. It's no good looking to them. You instinctively look to Jesus. In this case he's asleep. So of course you wake him up. He'll know what to do. He'll be your helper.

Now the Spirit has come as our advocate and helper. When you're flustered or panicked, you can tell yourself, "It's OK, the Spirit is with me". We can tell one another, "It's OK, the Spirit is our strengthener". When someone asks you a hard question about your faith, you can tell yourself, "It's OK, the Spirit is with me. He will testify as I speak. I don't need to convict and convince. That's the Spirit's job."

A few weeks ago I was thinking about a pastoral issue. "The worst of it is," I said to myself, "I'm having to face this alone because God isn't involved." I was full of self-pity. I wasn't, as it were, looking over my shoulder to see my advocate. I wasn't like the disciples, looking round to spot Jesus. I was just looking at the problem, and I felt as if I had to face it on my own. But I wasn't on my own; my advocate was with me. When the time came to meet up with those involved, I found myself looking on as the problem was resolved. I did nothing. My advocate did it all.

THE PRESENCE OF JESUS
But the Spirit is more than a replacement for Jesus. Look closely at what Jesus says:

> *I will not leave you as orphans;* ***I will come to you.***
> *Before long, the world will not see me any more, but you*
> *will see me. Because I live, you also will live. On that day*
> *you will realise that I am in my Father, and you are in me,*
> *and* ***I am in you.*** *Whoever has my commands and keeps*
> *them is the one who loves me. The one who loves me will be*
> *loved by my Father, and* ***I too will love them and show***
> ***myself to them.***   *(John 14 v 18-21)*

Jesus says the Father will send the Holy Spirit (v 16-17). But he also says, "*I* will come to you". Jesus says the Holy Spirit "lives with you and will be *in* you". But he also says, "*I* will be in you". He says, "The one who loves me will be loved by my Father, and I too will love them and *show myself to them*".

- "I will come to you" (14 v 18).
- "I am in you" (14 v 19).
- "I will show myself to [you]" (14 v 21).

Can you see what Jesus is saying? The coming of the Spirit is the coming of Jesus.

Jesus really has gone. He's physically absent. John 14 v 19 is clear: "Before long, the world will not see me any more." You can't meet Jesus in the flesh today. You can't shake his hand.

But you *can* have an encounter with him. You can meet him, hear him, know him and enjoy him. Jesus comes to his people through the Spirit. He's literally "with us in Spirit".

Again, we have to remember that God is one being. The Holy Spirit is the Spirit of Christ. He makes Christ present to us. In one sense, as we've seen, there are two advocates since the Spirit is "another" advocate. But in another sense there's only one advocate: Jesus-present-through-the-Spirit. It's not that Jesus has lost interest or handed on the job. Jesus himself is our strengthener and helper through the Holy Spirit.

Two images may help. First, think of an ambassador. An ambassador speaks on behalf of a monarch. They represent them in their absence. When an ambassador speaks in an official capacity, it's the voice of the monarch that is heard. In the same way, the Spirit is like an ambassador who speaks and acts on behalf of Christ. And because the Spirit fully knows the mind of Christ, his words and actions perfectly represent Christ's intentions towards us. We are back to the principle of three and one: because God is one, then an encounter with the Spirit is a real encounter with Jesus.

Second, think of a phone call. When we talk on the phone, we hear the very words of a distant friend. It's not another person. It's their own voice and their words are immediate. In the same way, the Spirit is like the technology that links us to Christ. He's the fibre-optic cable or wireless connection. So we hear the voice of Jesus. It's not another person. It's Jesus himself. And his words are immediate even though he's physically absent.

I was camping in the Cheviot Hills on the Scottish border a couple of years ago. At one point I was five miles from a road. Due to a slight miscalculation (which involved thinking I was 17 rather than 47), I was in a lot of pain. Then I went into shock and started shivering badly. I could have done with some help. I needed a strengthener and a helper. But I hadn't had any phone signal for the last seven or eight miles. I was completely out of range. Eventually I pitched my tent, warmed up in my sleeping bag and lived to tell the tale. But humanly speaking I was well and truly on my own.

Jesus has ascended to heaven. That's a long way away—we're talking other realms. But *he's not out of range*. He's connected to us by the Holy Spirit.

We need *both* these images because on their own neither does justice to the way the Spirit makes Christ real to us. The ambassador image captures its personal nature, but not the immediacy. The phone call captures the immediacy, but not the personal nature of the Spirit's work. The Spirit is a person, not an "it". At the same time, we really do hear the voice of Christ, not just his representative.

MEETING JESUS AROUND THE TABLE

"Christ is enough," we often say to one another. And that's true. But how is satisfaction in Christ to be tangible, to feel real? Or is satisfaction in Christ a mental exercise, maybe even an act of make-believe?

One of the words we use to describe the Lord's Supper is "communion". It's a biblical term. It comes from the King James Version of 1 Corinthians 10 v 16: "The cup of blessing which we bless, is it not the communion of the blood of Christ? The bread which we break, is it not the communion of the body of Christ?" It implies that the Lord's Supper is an act of communion or participation with Christ. It's a relational act.

Meals are often like that. Think of what an invitation to dinner means. It's more than an invitation to food. It's an invitation to friendship. Communion is an invitation to friendship with Christ: an invitation to enjoy and experience Christ's presence.

How is Christ present at communion? How can eating bread and drinking wine be an act of communion with Christ? The answer is that Christ is present by the Holy Spirit. He's not physically present, but he is spiritually present—present by the Spirit. We are lifted up to be with Christ. The Spirit collapses the distance between us.

So Christ really is present when we take communion. He is there to reassure us of his love, his protection, his commitment. The bread and wine are physical signs of his spiritual presence. Isn't Christ present with us by the Spirit all the time as he promised (Matthew 28 v 20)? Yes. But Christ in his kindness—knowing how frail we are, knowing how battered by life we can be—has given us bread and wine as physical signs of his presence.

Imagine a couple on the sofa watching television. As they sit together, he takes her hand in his. Or imagine you're sitting beside the hospital bed of a loved one and you take their hand in yours. Why? What does it add? Do they need this gesture to know that you're with them or that you love them or that you're for them? No. But it helps. It makes your presence physical, tangible, felt. It reassures them of your love. That's what happens at communion when Jesus offers us bread and wine. His presence and his love become tangible.

Baptism is like a wedding. Formal promises are made and commitments are given. As a result of a wedding, a single person becomes a married person. Our status changes. It's the same with baptism. Our status changes and we become in-Christ people. If baptism is like a wedding, then communion is like a kiss. It's the reaffirmation of love. Christ comes close to us to reassure us of his love. He comes close to kiss us.

Consider a wife who's had an argument with her husband or let him down in some way. What does she want? She wants him to take her in his arms and tell her that he loves her. And perhaps she needs both the physical touch and the reassuring words. Touch without words or words without touch could feel superficial, hesitant, as if he's still withholding his affection. And so it is that Jesus gives us both words and touch.

Think back to the last time you celebrated communion. In our church, we normally celebrate it in our home groups, perhaps around the dining table or in the lounge. You all have your own equivalent place where communion normally occurs. But this is what we've got to realise: as we take communion together, earth and heaven connect. Through the Spirit, the communion meal is a kind of gateway or portal to heaven. The Spirit connects us with Christ. He brings us into the presence of Christ.

This is what you have to see in your imagination with the eyes of faith. By "imagine" I don't mean "pretend", as if this is not real. I mean to see by faith the *spiritual* reality that is taking place. The table is Christ's table and he welcomes us to eat with him at his table.

Conversion could it be ?

PUTTING IT INTO PRACTICE

In Roman Catholicism the bread is called "the host" because it is supposed to "host" the physical presence of Christ. But in fact Christ himself is the host. He is the host who invites us to eat with him at his table. The people who serve are Jesus' way of getting the bread from the table into your hands. Think of it in those terms. When you take the plate, or the bread is put in your hands, think to yourself, "Jesus himself is giving me this bread. He is the host of this meal. This is his gift. This is a sign of his love. This is his kiss."

Did Neil Dickson allude to this?

ACTION *i.e. Sacrament: importance of*

When you take communion, imagine receiving the bread and wine as if from the hands of Jesus, as a sign of his love.

MIKE AND EMMA'S MONDAY MORNING

Yesterday God had felt so present to Mike. But today… today is different. Today is over-crowded trains, sweaty passengers, a wet shirt and the all-too-present void left by little Rosie. Today God is… What is he? Not absent—Mike doesn't doubt that God is everywhere. But God doesn't exactly feel present either. Not in a way he can touch or see.

"If only I could touch God," Mike thinks. And then he thinks about receiving the bread and wine at communion the day before. There was something he could touch. Here was Christ's promise in physical form. This was Christ's way of making his presence felt.

He thinks about the kiss he'd given his wife that morning. Last week he'd got a text from her as he sat on the train: "No kiss today. Still love me? Xx". He'd smiled and sent an emoji. "It'll do," she'd replied. It was a playful enough exchange, but he knew it mattered to her. That morning kiss was a sign of their love. He thought about the bread again. Here is a sign of Christ's love. A tangible touch.

REFLECTION QUESTIONS

- The previous chapter ended with a challenge to think of Jesus looking on with sympathy whenever you struggle. How have you got on? What difference has it made?
- Think back over the last week. Was there a moment when you felt the need for an advocate, strengthener, witness or helper?
- What difference would it have made to look over your shoulder and see (with the eyes of faith) Jesus present with you by the Spirit?
- How do you view communion? How could you approach it so that it has more meaning for you?
- Think of a time when a loving touch—a hug or a kiss or holding hands—has meant a lot to you. What difference would it make if you viewed communion as a loving touch from Jesus?

Regular employee huddle —
a sports team

Engaging. Focussing.
Communing with the
Lord ~

Reinforcing commitment
to the Lord.
A review meeting
collective response
collective communion
on the purpose/goal/
or on the altogether lovely one.
the beauty
enhancing our perception of the
Lord.

IN EVERY TEMPTATION WE CAN ENJOY THE SPIRIT'S LIFE

Let me tell you seven stories.

STORY ONE

"In the beginning God created the heavens and the earth. Now the earth was formless and empty, darkness was over the surface of the deep, and the Spirit of God was hovering over the waters" (Genesis 1 v 1-2). "Spirit," "breath" and "wind" are all the same word in Hebrew and Greek. So "the Wind of God" breathed out from God is blowing over the waters.

"And God said, 'Let there be light,' and there was light" (Genesis 1 v 3). God spoke and the world came into being. The writer of Psalm 33 says, "By the word of the LORD the heavens were made, their starry host by the breath of his mouth" (Psalm 33 v 6). The word of God comes on the breath of God bringing light and life and beauty. God separates and orders. He separates light from dark. He separates the waters to create dry land, and fills that land with vegetation and animals.

Then God shapes the dust into a human form. But it's lifeless—like a shop mannequin—until God "breathed into his nostrils the breath of life [or the Spirit of life], and the man became a living being" (Genesis 2 v 7). "All creatures look to you," says Psalm 104 v 27-30, and "when you take away their breath, they die and return to the dust. When you send your Spirit, they are created, and you renew the face of the ground." The Spirit animates all creation. Everything has life through the Spirit.

STORY TWO

By the time we get to Noah, humanity is deeply wicked. So God sends death in the form of a flood. Noah and his family are left floating in the ark on an endless ocean, surrounded by death. There appears to be no prospect for terrestrial life. But then God "sent a wind over the earth, and the waters receded" (Genesis 8 v 1). This is the story of creation all over again. The Wind or Spirit of God blows over the waters to separate the waters and land again to give hope for life.

STORY THREE

Fast-forward in the story. God's people have been enslaved by the Egyptians. But God has sent ten plagues and the Egyptians have freed God's people. But now Pharaoh has changed his mind and sent his army to recapture them. God's people are cornered. In front of them is the sea. Behind them is the Egyptian army. "Then Moses stretched out his hand over the sea, and all that night the LORD drove the sea back with a strong east wind and turned it into dry land. The waters were divided [or separated], and the Israelites went through the sea on dry ground, with a wall of water on their right and on their left" (Exodus 14 v 21-22). It's the same story again. The Wind or the Spirit of God is blowing across the waters, separating the waters to create dry ground. The Spirit leads God's people to life and freedom.

STORY FOUR

The Spirit of God sets the prophet Ezekiel in the middle of a valley. As Ezekiel stands there, all around him are dry bones—skulls, vertebra, sterna, ribs, clavicles, scapulae, pelvises, femurs, tibias. The bones represent God's spiritually dead people.

Ezekiel is told to prophesy: "Dry bones, hear the word of the LORD!" (Ezekiel 37 v 4). The bones come together, flesh forms on them and skin covers them. "But there was no breath in them" (Ezekiel 37 v 8). They're like the lifeless lump of clay in Eden. Ezekiel is surrounded by inanimate clay forms, like the Terracotta Army of the first Chinese Emperor.

So God tells Ezekiel to "prophesy to the breath". He's to call on the Breath or the Spirit of God. I imagine Ezekiel feeling a gentle breeze, a gust of wind on his cheeks. Then gradually it increases in strength until a mighty wind is blowing through the valley—the Wind of God. God breathes the Breath of life. "And breath entered them; they came to life and stood up on their feet—a vast army" (Ezekiel 37 v 10).

STORY FIVE

Fast-forward again to the first century AD and enter a tomb. There in the gloom you see the dead body of Jesus. Psalm 104 said, "When you take away their breath, they die and return to the dust" (Psalm 104 v 29). There before you is the body of Jesus returning to the dust—a lifeless, rotting corpse.

And then the Spirit or the Wind of God blows through the tomb and breathes life into the body of Jesus (Romans 1 v 4; 8 v 11). The heart starts to beat again. The lungs draw in breath. The eyes open. The Word that was silenced on the hill at Calvary speaks again.

STORY SIX

Later that day Jesus appears to his followers. "As the Father has sent me," he says, "I am sending you". Then Jesus breathes on them, saying, "Receive the Holy Spirit" (John 20 v 21-22). The Son of God breathes the Breath or Spirit of God into the fearful, powerless hearts of his followers. It's a picture of what will happen seven weeks later when a violent wind blows through the building where the disciples are gathered (Acts 2). It's the Wind, the Breath, the Spirit of God. Tongues of flame appear over their heads and they praise God in the languages of many nations. They are filled with power to proclaim Jesus as Lord and Saviour.

A few days later the authorities tell them to stop evangelising, so they gather to pray. "Enable your servants to speak your word with great boldness," they pray (Acts 4 v 29). "After they prayed, the place where they were meeting was shaken." The Wind of God again blows through the building. "And they were all filled with the Holy Spirit and spoke the word of God boldly" (Acts 4 v 31).

STORY SEVEN

Forty years ago I was dead. You wouldn't know it to look at me—I was a young child, full of life. But spiritually I was dead. I didn't need a more persuasive argument or a more moving meeting. I was dead. I needed an act of resurrection or rebirth.

Then one evening I was talking to my mother about Jesus. I wanted to follow him. So she called for my father and together we prayed. The room didn't shake. There was no violent wind. But the Spirit or Breath of God had breathed new life into my heart. I was reborn. I was resurrected.

If you're a Christian, then you have a similar story to tell. The details may be very different. But at the heart of your conversion was an act of the Holy Spirit. The Spirit breathed life into your dead heart. He opened your blind eyes to the glory of Christ. He gave you the gift of faith.

RAISING OUR EXPECTATIONS

What are your expectations of the Spirit of God?

There are two dangers. There are people who expect *too much*. They expect the glory of heaven now in this life. They expect health and wealth and fun. Often people have said to me, "God has told me he wants to give me this". In reality it's just a projection of their own selfish desires. They want glory without the cross, without sacrifice, without suffering. But Paul told new churches, "We must go through many hardships to enter the kingdom of God" (Acts 14 v 22). Jesus said, "Whoever wants to be my disciple must deny themselves and take up their cross and follow me" (Mark 8 v 34). That's one danger—expecting now what belongs to the life to come.

But there's a second danger, and I suspect that for many of us this is closer to home. It's the danger of expecting *too little*. We try to take the supernatural out of our Christianity. But Christianity is not simply a set of beliefs. It's a dynamic relationship with the living God. The Spirit, the Breath, the Wind of God still blows through his people. It may not be accompanied by shaking buildings or violent winds, but the Spirit still comes to bring life, power and courage.

The advantage of expecting little from God is that little is expected from you. "I can't do that." "I can't invite my colleagues." "We can't plant a new church." The pastor and author Francis Chan says:

> *I don't want my life to be explainable without the Holy Spirit ... I don't believe God wants me (or any of his children) to live in a way that makes sense from the world's perspective, a way I know I can "manage" ...*

> *If we never pray audacious, courageous prayers, how can*
> *he answer them? If we never follow him to positions where*
> *we need him, how can he show up and make his presence*
> *known? ...*
>
> *No matter where you live and what your days look like,*
> *you have the choice each day to depend on yourself, to live*
> *safely, and to try to control your life. Or you can live as*
> *you were created to live—as a temple of the Holy Spirit*
> *of God, as a person dependent on him, desperate for God*
> *the Spirit to show up and make a difference.*[40]

It may be that we rarely experience the Spirit of God because we never need him. Our lives are too secure. Our prayers are too safe. Our expectations are too low.

The key is not to "balance" our expectations—"not too much, not too little"; the key is to recognise why the Spirit gives life and power. He gives power to proclaim Christ and he gives life so we might die to self. And you can't have too much of that kind of power and life.

NEW DESIRES AND NEW POWER

Paul emphasises the life-giving work of the Spirit in Romans 8. The Spirit gives *spiritual* life in the present (v 5-8) and *physical* life in the future (v 9-11).

> [5] *Those who live according to the flesh have their minds set*
> *on what the flesh desires; but those who live in accordance*
> *with the Spirit have their minds set on what the Spirit*
> *desires.* [6] *The mind governed by the flesh is death, but the*
> *mind governed by the Spirit is life and peace.* [7] *The mind*
> *governed by the flesh is hostile to God; it does not submit*
> *to God's law, nor can it do so.* [8] *Those who are in the realm*
> *of the flesh cannot please God.*

> *⁹ You, however, are not in the realm of the flesh but are in the realm of the Spirit, if indeed the Spirit of God lives in you. And if anyone does not have the Spirit of Christ, they do not belong to Christ. ¹⁰ But if Christ is in you, then even though your body is subject to death because of sin, the Spirit gives life because of righteousness. ¹¹ And if the Spirit of him who raised Jesus from the dead is living in you, he who raised Christ from the dead will also give life to your mortal bodies because of his Spirit who lives in you.* (Romans 8 v 5-11)

"The Spirit gives life" says verse 10. Here's the amazing thing: the same Spirit who raised Christ from the dead "*lives in you*" (v 11). The Spirit who breathed life into the rotting flesh of Jesus is the Spirit who breathes life into your heart. You already have resurrection power coursing through your veins.

If I asked you when you last experienced the power of the Spirit, I wonder how you would reply. Perhaps you're thinking, "I'm not sure I can ever remember performing a miracle or speaking in some kind of anointed way". But left to ourselves we would be living for self in proud defiance of God. So *all* the good we do is done in the power of the Spirit.

- When you have faith in Christ, you're enjoying the Spirit's life.
- When you willingly serve God, you're enjoying the Spirit's life.
- When you joyfully sacrifice for Christ, you're enjoying the Spirit's life.
- When you have any affection for your Christian brothers and sisters, you're enjoying the Spirit's life.
- When you recoil from sin, you're enjoying the Spirit's life.

- When you have any desire for holiness, you're
  enjoying the Spirit's life.

Through the Spirit you can do something today that brings
God pleasure. I wonder if you believe that. Or I wonder
if you think, "Even the good things I try to do are tainted
by sin. I do them, but then I feel pride. Or I do them out
of guilt." Maybe you imagine God looking on and thinking, "What a pathetic attempt at righteousness". It's true
that those "in the realm of the flesh cannot please God"
(Romans 8 v 8). But, if you're a Christian, you're not in the
realm of the flesh. You're in the realm of the Spirit. And so
you can bring God pleasure.

What you do may not be perfect. But God will look on
you as a father looks on a small child. We have pictures in
our home that small children have drawn for us—scribbles
that need a word of parental explanation at the bottom. I'll
not mention who the artists are, but they're all rubbish! But
we still hang them in our home because as honorary parents we regard them as beautiful. A loving father delights in
his children, despite all their failings. And there is no father
more loving than our heavenly Father.

But this image only captures half the reality that is ours
in Christ. We also have reproductions of great artworks in
our home—created by people who were inspired to produce great works of art. Christians, too, are inspired by the
Holy Spirit. And so now we're capable of producing great
works of love that truly are magnificent.

When you risk hostility to speak of Christ, or when you
choose to attend a prayer meeting on a cold night, or when
you decide to spend time with someone in need, or when you
do any little act of sacrifice for Christ, then you experience
the life of the Spirit in you. It may not be anything dramatic.
There's probably no tingle down the spine or warm glow in

your heart. But you know that left to yourself you would be selfish, and any good you might do would actually be done out of pride. But God in his grace doesn't leave you to yourself. He sends his Spirit to give new life and new desires.

In this life Christians experience our new Spirit-inspired desires alongside our old, lingering selfish desires (Galatians 5 v 16-17). So we often experience the life of the Spirit in the form of struggle. We're pulled in two directions. When we're tempted to do wrong, the Spirit pulls us back to God. When we're led by the Spirit to do right, our old selfish desires pull us back to sin. But that struggle is itself a sign of the Spirit's work.

A couple of years ago we paid off our mortgage. Our house used to belong to the bank and now it belongs to us. But all that happened on that day was that someone in the Land Registry Office deleted the words "Leeds Building Society" on a computer and replaced them with "Tim and Helen Chester". Back at home nothing changed. Maybe that's how you think about becoming a Christian. Maybe you think it only really occurs somewhere off in an office in heaven. You're moved from one list to another. But back on earth nothing really changes.

Nothing could be further from the truth. It's much more like a developer who buys a house and then sends in a one-person renovation force. Christ has bought you with his own blood and now he's sent in the Holy Spirit to renovate you. The blueprint that the Spirit is working to is Jesus himself. God is working so that we might "be conformed to the image of his Son" (Romans 8 v 29).

This means *you don't have to sin*. There's nothing inevitable about it. I wonder if there's a sin that you feel powerless to change.[41] Maybe the temptation grows so strong you feel unable to resist. Maybe it creeps up and takes you by surprise so that before you know it you've reacted badly.

You've tried to change many times. But you just feel struck. The Nicene Creed says, "We believe in the Holy Spirit, the Lord, the giver of life". If you're in Christ, then the Spirit has given you life: life to live for God, life to change old habits, life to proclaim Christ's name. You have new desires, new life, new power.

There is nothing that God expects you to do that you cannot do. The sin that defeats you need not defeat you. The fears that consume you need not consume you. The people who terrify you need not terrify you. You have the Spirit of life within you empowering you to know God and follow Christ.

So don't give up the struggle with sin. Re-engage in the battle. Having described the life-giving work of the Spirit in Romans 8, Paul continues, "Therefore, brothers and sisters, we have an obligation ... by the Spirit ... put to death the misdeeds of the body" (8 v 12-13). We no longer have a loyalty to the old family—to humanity in Adam under the reign of sin. Our loyalty now is to our new family—to humanity in Christ led by the Spirit. So let's do battle with sin. Let's kill it.

Every time you're tempted to explode in rage, or go off in a sulk, or make it all about you, or find refuge in porn, or exaggerate to impress others—in all these situations and many more you can enjoy communion with the Holy Spirit. *In every temptation you can enjoy the life of the Spirit.* You can engage in the battle with a conscious sense of dependence on the Spirit. You can know the Spirit's power as you resist the pull of your sinful desires. All you need to do is say "No" to sin and "Yes" to God.

PUTTING IT INTO PRACTICE

I wonder if some of us don't "feel" the work of the Spirit because we're not on the frontline—we're not on the frontline of the battle against sin or we're not on the frontline of the battle for mission.

Imagine you've been driving a small car with a beat-up engine which struggles to go much over 30 mph. Then one day someone gives you a powerful new car with a large turbo-charged engine. A week later you shock them by saying, "I haven't really noticed much difference". But then they discover that you've never driven it over 30 mph. You've got this car that can accelerate to 70 mph in three seconds. But you don't notice the difference because you've never hit the accelerator. Some of us don't "feel" the power of the Spirit because we've never hit the accelerator. Don't make your life so safe that you never have cause to notice the Spirit's work.

How do we live in communion with the Holy Spirit? We rely on him. We expect him to work. If you want to see the Spirit at work in your life, then attempt things that you feel you can't do without his help. Everything we do for God is done with the Spirit's help, whether we feel it or not. But if you want to feel the Spirit's help, then attempt things that feel beyond you. Do not complain that God never does anything dramatic in your life if you never attempt anything outside your comfort zone.

ACTION
Take a risk for God this week.

It might be inviting a neighbour to church, declaring your allegiance to Christ in the workplace, offering to pray with an unbeliever, being extravagantly generous with your time or money—something that makes you feel your dependence on the Spirit's help.

MIKE AND EMMA'S MONDAY MORNING
Emma's standing in the playground, chatting to other mums while Poppy pulls on her shirt. "Have you heard about Roxanne? You know, Jamal's mum? Well, I've heard…"

Emma's not heard. She wants to. A bit of gossip to spice up her morning. A bit of scandal to make her feel superior. She moves in so she can hear better.

"No," she says to herself. "Don't go there. Bad idea." She turns round. Was it a bad idea? What harm would come of a little gossip? It would distract from the tedium of the day. But Emma thinks of God's word. She thinks of Christ's grace to her. She wants to show the same grace to others. "Sorry," she shouts over her shoulder, "I need to dash." Nobody notices. They're all huddled round the latest rumour.

She smiles. She's said no to temptation. She's thinks back a few years. In another life she'd be known as "the Gossip Queen". But not anymore. Not since she's become a Christian. Of course, she's still tempted to join in. But something's changed. It's one of those things she never notices from day to day—like Poppy getting taller. But looking back over a few months she can see the Holy Spirit at work in her heart. "God is changing me," Emma thinks. "Wow!"

REFLECTION QUESTIONS

- The previous chapter ended with an invitation to receive the bread and wine as if from the hands of Jesus as a sign of his love. How have you got on? What difference has this made?
- Is there a "Story 8" that you could add to the seven stories of the Spirit in this chapter?
- Is your danger expecting the glory of heaven now or expecting too little from the Spirit?
- Think of some of the ways you no longer desire sin and some of the ways you now want to please God. Each of these is a mighty work of the Spirit in your life.
- Has there been a moment recently when you felt the need of the Spirit's help? What's the evidence in your life that you're depending on God?

IN EVERY GROAN
WE CAN ENJOY
THE SPIRIT'S HOPE

N ow I've hit 50 I can't stand up without groaning. Any physical exertion is accompanied by a little exhalation of breath. *Oooph*. You get the idea.

Into my 40s I used to play soccer with men half my age. Or were they boys? I could read the game so much better than ever I used to. But sadly I lacked the speed, strength and energy to play the pass I could see in my mind. I used to comfort myself with the thought that my teammates would never be better than they were now in their early 20s, but they didn't know how good I was in my prime. Not very good, as it happens, but they didn't know that! If no one had booked the pitch after us, we had the option of playing on. They were usually all for carrying on. But after 60 minutes I was more than ready to drag my old body home to a cup of tea and a warm bath.

My body is ageing. And the more I age, the more I groan.

But then my groans are fairly minor and mostly self-inflicted. Laura groans because multiple sclerosis is destroying her body ahead of time. Colin groans because his wife is dying of cancer. Abdul groans as his homeland is torn apart by civil war. Jemma quietly groans the loss of her miscarried child. What communion with God do we enjoy in the midst of our groaning?

Every prayer to the Father is a mighty miracle as "the Spirit himself testifies with our spirit that we are God's children" (Romans 8 v 16). Yet, as we saw in chapter 5, the miracle of confidence before God is so mighty that most of the time we hardly notice what a miracle it is! The Spirit of God enables us to share the experience of sonship that God the Son experiences (v 14-16). That's a glorious gift of grace that brings confidence, intimacy and joy. But we're not spared the sufferings and frustrations of life. Paul continues in Romans 8 v 17, "Now if we are children, then we are heirs—heirs of God and co-heirs with Christ, if indeed we share in his sufferings in order that we may also share in his glory". We will share the Son's experience of glory, but we also share his experience of suffering.

Yet something astonishing is happening every time we groan.

CREATION GROANS

First, Paul says all creation groans with us. "The whole creation has been groaning as in the pains of childbirth" (Romans 8 v 22). Our cries are an echo of a creation that has been "subjected to frustration" (v 18-21). The world around us feels the curse of sin.

My daughter was part of a team that curated an exhibition of contemporary art in the Courtauld Gallery in London. One exhibit featured a phone which, when you picked it up, linked directly to a microphone embedded in a glacier. What you heard was the creak and groans as sheets of ice rubbed against one another. I immediately thought of Paul's description of creation groaning with frustration.

But creation has been subjected to frustration *"in hope"* (v 20). A day is coming when it will be "liberated from its bondage to decay and brought into the freedom and glory of the children of God" (v 21). Paul imagines the natural world as a child on tiptoes, eagerly expecting her father to come home. Or like a woman in labour, groaning in pain but joyfully anticipating the delivery of her child. Isaiah does something similar. He imagines the mountains bursting into song and the trees breaking into applause when the time of creation's renewal comes (Isaiah 55 v 12). Creation groans, but it groans in eager expectation.

WE GROAN

And this is our experience too. We, too, groan in expectation. "Not only so," says Paul, "but we ourselves, who have the firstfruits of the Spirit, groan inwardly as we wait eagerly for our adoption to sonship, the redemption of our bodies" (v 23). Creation "waits in eager expectation" in verse 19 and "we wait eagerly" in verse 23. Creation is "groaning" in verse 22 and we "groan inwardly" in verse 23.

We may have been adopted and have the Spirit of adoption, but our bodies are not yet redeemed. We feel the brokenness of the world, often in our own bodies, and we groan. We are broken people living in a broken world.

WE GROAN WITH *LONGING*

But here's the difference the Spirit makes. For most people groaning is *a backwards look*. Things are not the way they were. They're not the way they should be. We live in a broken world. Even unbelievers sense this. Unbelievers lament the fact that the world is not what it should be. Unbelievers groan.

But for Christians groaning is also *a forwards look*. We know that things are not the way they *will* be. And this is the Spirit's work. It's "we … who have the firstfruits of the Spirit" who groan (8 v 23). Everyone groans. But only Christians groan because we're looking forward, eagerly waiting to be brought into our new, adopted home. We groan because we have the Holy Spirit, the firstfruits of that redeemed creation.

The Spirit makes us long for the new creation in two ways. First, because he gives us an experience of new creation. He's described as the "firstfruits". He's the taster or trial sample. It's like a cook preparing a grand meal who offers you a spoonful of casserole. And the beautiful taste of that spoonful fills you with longing for the full banquet.

WE GROAN AS *CHILDREN*

Second, the Spirit makes us long for the new creation because he makes us think of it as home. When I travel, I always look forward to coming home again. Why? Because it's where my family is. Think what happens as the Spirit testifies to us that we are God's children? That God the Father is our Father? Our home changes. Home for us is no longer this passing world. Now home is God's coming world. Home is where our family is. At the moment that's heaven. But one day heaven and earth will be united in a new creation in which God makes his dwelling (Revelation 21 v 1-5).

The author and theologian Russell Moore describes how he was struck by the terrible, poignant silence of the Russian orphanage. Children learn not to cry out when no one comes to them—when no one cares for them. For a week Moore and his wife played with their two future sons. They read to them, sang to them, held them, loved them. And each evening they walked out leaving this eerie silence behind. And then on the last day the time came for them to go. They had to go back to the United States to complete the legal formalities before the boys could become part of their family. And Moore says he felt compelled to turn back. He went back in and, quoting the words of Jesus, said, "We will not leave you as orphans. We will come for you." And as they walked out down the corridor, they heard one of their sons scream out. The scream of a one-year-old—wordless, angry and desperate. And Moore says it was the most terrible and lovely thing he ever heard. It cut him to the heart, but it was the cry of a son for his father. With that cry of anguish, this orphan had become a son.[42]

The Spirit testifies with our spirit that we are God's children (v 16). But that experience of adoption is still partial. Creation is not yet liberated; our bodies are not yet redeemed. So "we wait eagerly for our adoption to sonship" (v 23). Our experience of sonship makes us long for more. It adds to every pain, every sin and every loss a sense of longing. We know there's more to come.

By the Spirit "we cry, '*Abba*, Father'" (8 v 15). The word translated "cry" is a strong word. It's not a gentle or affectionate word to be softly spoken. It's a cry for help. We were walking with friends once when their daughter fell through the ice into the river. "Daaad!" she screamed in shock and fear. Her father jumped into the icy waters without a second's thought to pull her out. That's what the "*Abba*, Father" cry is—a desperate cry for help that makes a father come running.

The only time in the Gospels when Jesus says, "*Abba*, Father" is in Gethsemane as he sweats blood (Mark 14 v 36; Luke 22 v 44). Jesus was about to bear the brokenness of the world and he cried out, "*Abba*, Father". And when we feel that brokenness in our own lives, the Spirit prompts us to cry out, "*Abba*, Father". Every groan becomes an invitation to whisper, "Father".

THE SPIRIT GROANS

People often assume experiencing the Spirit equates to spine-tingling moments of ecstasy. And indeed such experiences can be the work of the Spirit. But Paul goes on in Romans 8 v 26 to say "the Spirit helps us in our weakness". If you've ever gone through a dark time and come out the other side—that was an experience of the Spirit. If you've ever doubted everything you ever knew about the Christian faith, but somehow kept praying—that was an experience of the Spirit.

But then Paul goes one astonishing step further. He says the Spirit himself "groans" (v 26). Creation groans; we groan; and the Spirit groans. Creation groans because it's subject to frustration. We groan because we feel the brokenness of the world in our lives, often in our own bodies. God is not frustrated, nor is he broken; but through the Spirit, he feels our pain with us. Every groan we utter is echoed by the Spirit.

And when the pain seems too much and our words run out, the Spirit continues on our behalf.

> *We do not know what we ought to pray for, but the Spirit himself intercedes for us through wordless groans.*
> *(Romans 8 v 26)*

When you feel as if you're rowing through life with energy like an Olympic oarsman, hurtling towards the finishing line, it's the Spirit who's pulsing through your veins. But also, when you're too weak to row and you feel that you're just drifting, it's the Spirit who comes as a gentle breeze to nudge you home.

God will answer the Spirit's prayer because by this point we're in a wonderfully circular process. The Spirit's groans may be wordless, but the Father knows what the Spirit has in mind, and what the Spirit has in mind perfectly matches the will of the Father. "He who searches our hearts knows the mind of the Spirit, because the Spirit intercedes for God's people in accordance with the will of God" (v 27). And that will is that we become like his Son (v 29). Your groan is taken up by the Spirit and presented to the Father in a form that matches the Father's purpose of making you like his Son. As a result, "in all things God works for the good of those who love him" (v 28).

The long and short of it is this: the Spirit transforms and transfigures our groans so they become part of the means by which God achieves his purposes in our lives. And God's great purpose is to make us like his glorious, beautiful Son.

PUTTING IT INTO PRACTICE

John Calvin commends what he calls the "meditation on the future life".[43] He has in mind a kind of spiritual discipline. We're to make time to think about the future God promises us—the renewal of creation, the redemption of our bodies and our adoption as children. We're to remind one another of the "eternal glory" that awaits us. We're to view our troubles from this perspective so that by comparison they seem "light and momentary" (2 Corinthians 4 v 17-18). We're to remember we're pilgrims passing through this world en route to "a better country" (Hebrews 11 v 13-16; 1 Peter 1 v 1; 2 v 11). "Although believers are now pilgrims on earth," says Calvin, "yet by their confidence they surmount the heavens, so that they cherish their future inheritance in their bosoms with tranquillity."[44] What frees us from the vain pursuit of earthly treasure is the hope of treasure in heaven (Matthew 6 v 19-20; 1 Timothy 6 v 17-19).

Meditating on the future life is something we could do on a regular basis, perhaps as part of our regular Bible-reading and prayer. But it's also something we can do whenever

[handwritten margin note: when we see Christ – one glimpse of His glory 2 when we see Christ dear face all sorrow will erase]

[handwritten note: Fairest Lord Jesus]

[handwritten note: Pilgrims . view]

we groan. *Every groan* you utter—from the sigh you make getting out of a chair to the aching void of bereavement—*is an invitation to enjoy the hope of the Spirit.* For some of us that adds up to many opportunities each day—many opportunities to look forward with eager expectation.

ACTION

Each day this week spend time thinking about eternal life in the new creation.

MIKE AND EMMA'S MONDAY MORNING

The train is slowly coming to a halt. Mike ducks down to look out the window, hoping to see the station platform coming into view. But all he sees is a wall of graffiti. "As a result of signal failure we'll be subject to a 15-minute delay. We apologise for any inconvenience this may cause." Mike lets out an audible groan. He's not the only one. The carriage comes alive with shared grumbles.

How long would this go on for? A fifteen-minute delay. A ten-minute walk to the office. What was the time now? He'd be at his desk by 9.10 perhaps. Then it would be over. Until the journey home. Until tomorrow. Until retirement. Another forty years of standing in this train. It felt like for ever.

Was this how things were meant to be? No. This is a broken world, Mike thinks. And, truth be told, commuting isn't the worst thing—not by a long way. But it will end. One day Christ will return and make all things new. Will there be commuting in the new creation? Probably not, Mike thinks. Or, if there is, it won't be like this. He looks round the carriage: at people whose only hope is a healthy retirement. "Holy Spirit," he says, "thank you for reminding me of the wonderful hope I have".

REFLECTION QUESTIONS

- The previous chapter ended with a challenge to take a risk for God. How have you got on?
- When do you find yourself groaning—audibly or inwardly?
- Think of a recent time when you groaned. How was your groan a reminder that this world is not what it will be? How will the reason for your groan be transformed in the new creation?
- Think about a difficult time in your life. Think about the ways in which the Holy Spirit helped you through.
- When did you last think about eternal life with Jesus in the new creation? What difference did it make to your attitude at the time?

IN EVERY WORD
WE CAN ENJOY
THE SPIRIT'S VOICE

"Shall we pray?" It's one of those questions to which
you can't really say no—"No, I don't want to pray. I've
got better things to do." We know that's the wrong thing to
say! Yet the reality is we don't often delight to read our Bi-
bles and pray. We're all for praying in a crisis. But praying first
thing in the morning with a list of tasks stretching ahead of
us... Well, we'd rather get on with the day. Or what about late
at night? We opt to switch off the light and go to sleep.

The key issue is not how you organise your time. We all
find time for what really matters to us. The issue is how
you think about reading your Bible and praying. It's all too
easy to think of them as primarily about a transfer of information. We read our Bible hoping to learn some new truth
about God that will add to the sum total of our knowledge.
And we pray to convey information to God: a list of things
we'd like him to do. But reading the Bible and praying are
much more than this. And if we can embrace that "more",
then we'll look forward to them with anticipation. The
secret is to see them as opportunities to enjoy a relationship
with God.

The Bible is a relational book. Its purpose is to create and deepen our relationship with God. It's not a quick reference tool. It's a place in which we hang out with God and get to know him. Imagine I come home and my wife starts telling me about her day. Imagine I interrupt with the words, "Can I stop you there? Just give me a couple of summary points. I've got other things I want to get on with." That wouldn't be a recipe for a good marriage! Conversations are not just about conveying information. They're also about building relationships. The Bible is no different. It's not a book to raid for a few facts about God. It's a means of communion.

MEANS OF COMMUNION

Some Christians talk about "spiritual disciplines". Spiritual disciplines are all the things we do that help us grow as Christians—things like prayer, Bible-reading, church life and so on. I'm all for spiritual disciplines. But I don't like the term. I'm not going to fight anyone over it or tell you off for using it. But I think there's a better term. The danger is that the language of spiritual disciplines makes my relationship with God something I achieve through my hard work. Nor do they sound like something I might want to do. I can think of spiritual disciplines as a kind of spiritual workout regime to enable me to be a self-made godly person. Sometimes that's attractive because it panders to our pride. But when we don't measure up, it can be crushing.

So traditionally many Christians have preferred to speak of "the means of grace". This is a big improvement. The means of grace are the things God graciously uses to draw us close to himself and make us like his Son. One advantage of this terminology is that it includes not only things we do (like prayer and Bible-reading), but also what happens to us (like baptism and suffering).

But the main advantage of the language of "means of grace" is that it moves the emphasis away from my achievement and back towards God's grace. Growth in Christ and intimacy with God are not something I achieve through the discipline of my will. Rather, they are something God achieves in me through the means of grace which he's provided. There's a clue in the name! It's all about God's grace. My responsibility is simply to make the most of these gifts.

But I suggest we go a step further. A danger with talking about the "means of grace" is that it can make them appear somewhat mechanistic, as if grace is a pill I receive. I've even heard them described as the delivery systems God uses to bring spiritual blessings to people on earth. This sounds like an automated snack-dispenser: you put your money in the slot, press the right button and a snack drops into the tray at the bottom. And if I read my Bible and pray, it seems, an appropriate quota of grace will be delivered to me.

But grace is not a "thing". You can't parcel it up and deliver it to someone. Grace is God's love towards those who don't deserve his love. It's profoundly relational. So grace can't be separated from God any more than I can parcel up some of my love and hand it to the postman to deliver somewhere else.

I suggest we use the term "means of communion". Prayer, community, worship, service and suffering are all means that God gives us to enjoy and deepen our *relationship* with him. In fact, every chapter in this book has focused on a means of communion. Every pleasure is a potential means of communion if you see it as a sign of your Father's generosity. Every pain is a potential means of communion if you see it as a sign of your Father's discipline. Every prayer, every failure, every fear, every supper, every temptation and every groan has the potential to draw us closer to God if we see God at work in it. The key is faith. Faith sees in all the ordinary things of life the extraordinary work of God. It might be birdsong or a headache or an angry word—all things that might easily go unnoticed. But faith sees them as God's means of communion, opportunities to respond to him—to thank God for birdsong, to accept the headache as formative or to trust that Christ has paid the price of the angry word.

HEARING GOD'S VOICE

What difference does it make when we view the Bible as a means of communion with God?[45]

Hebrews 3 v 7 says, "So, as the Holy Spirit says: 'Today, if you hear his voice…'" It's a quote from Psalm 95, written around 1,000 years before the writer of Hebrews sat down to pen his letter. A few verses later, Hebrews 4 v 7 introduces the same quotation by saying that God "spoke through David". The psalm has two authors: the Holy Spirit and King David. The words we read in the Bible are human words, but they're simultaneously divine words. God himself spoke the words we read. Paul describes them as "God-breathed" (2 Timothy 3 v 16). Peter says the writers of the Bible "spoke from God as they were carried along by the Holy Spirit" (2 Peter 1 v 21). In the Bible that you hold in your hands are the very words of God.

When did God last speak to you? The answer is a moment ago when you read 2 Peter 1 v 21. Look again at Hebrews 3 v 7. It doesn't say the Holy Spirit "spoke" these words. Instead it says, "as the Holy Spirit *says*". It's describing an event that's taking place in the present as the words are being read. God spoke in the Bible, but God also *speaks* in the Bible. The Bible isn't just a record of what once happened and what was once said. When the Bible is read, something happens. When the Bible is read or preached, God speaks. *In every word we can enjoy the Spirit's voice.* Right here, right now.

As it happens, the quote that Hebrews 3 v 7 introduces reinforces this idea: "Today, if you hear his voice do not harden your hearts". Psalm 95 recalls two stories from the exodus from Egypt in which the people of Israel grumbled against God. Several centuries on, David takes God's words spoken back at the exodus and invites his readers to hear them afresh "today". *Today God is speaking to you*, he says in effect. Another thousand years on and the writer of Hebrews does the same thing. "Today ... hear his voice." And when we read the letter of Hebrews, it happens yet again, a further 2,000 years on. "Today ... hear his voice."

"For the word of God is alive and active." That's the conclusion of Hebrews 4 v 12. The Bible is an accurate record of what God has said and done. But it's more than that. It's alive. It's the living voice of God. "The Spirit that worked in the hearts of the *writers* of the Bible to ensure what they *wrote* was God's word is the same Spirit that works in the hearts of *readers* of the Bible to ensure what we *hear* is God's word."[46]

The Bible is also *active*. It's doing something. It's busy. God is at work when the Bible is read. At creation God spoke, and through his words he brought order, light and life. And today when God speaks through his word, he orders the chaos of our lives, brings light to our darkness and creates life in dead hearts. Or consider what God's word does according to Psalm 19 v 7-13:

> *The law of the* Lord *is perfect,*
> *refreshing the soul.*
> *The statutes of the* Lord *are trustworthy,*
> *making wise the simple.*
> *The precepts of the* Lord *are right,*
> *giving joy to the heart.*
> *The commands of the* Lord *are radiant,*
> *giving light to the eyes ...*

By them your servant is warned;
in keeping them there is great reward.
But who can discern their own errors?
Forgive my hidden faults.
Keep your servant also from wilful sins;
may they not rule over me.
Then will I be blameless,
innocent of great transgression.

The Bible refreshes the soul, makes us wise, gives joy to the heart, enlightens our eyes, warns us against error, exposes our faults and liberates us from sin. That's quite an agenda. But then this word is *God's* word.

KNOWING GOD'S PRESENCE

Seen and not heard. That supposedly was what the Victorians thought children should be. In the Bible story the opposite is true of God. He is heard and not seen. Time and again he directly intervenes in the life of his people. But he intervenes not by appearing, but by speaking. What Moses said of the encounter with God at Mount Sinai is actually the norm: "You heard the sound of words but saw no form; there was only a voice" (Deuteronomy 4 v 12). The LORD refused to show his glory to Moses "for no one may see me and live" (Exodus 33 v 20). Instead God came to Moses hidden in a cloud and revealed his Name (Exodus 34 v 5-6).

Is God absent from the story because he can't be seen? No, clearly not. He's present and active through his words. Is God absent from your life because you can't see him? No. He's present and active in your life through his words. Nor is he present through a substitute. It's not that he's sent a representative to convey his word. He's personally present in his word through the person of the Holy Spirit.

Imagine a child who wakes in the middle of the night. She can see nothing in the darkness so she cries out in fear. Then she hears her father's voice. He speaks words of comfort. His words reassure her and a few moments later she drops back off to sleep. What did she see? Nothing. Yet she was reassured that her father was there because she heard his voice. The same thing happens when we read the Bible. What do we see? Nothing. But we experience God's presence as we hear his voice. John Calvin said:

> *If our Lord is so good to us as to have his doctrine still preached to us, we have by that a sure and infallible sign that he is near at hand to us, that he seeks our salvation, that he calls us to himself as though he spoke with open mouth, and that we see him personally before us … Jesus Christ … holds out his arms to receive us, as often as the gospel is preached to us.*[47]

The apostle John wants us to share his fellowship with the Father and the Son. This is what brings him joy—to see people enjoying communion with God. But what does John do to make this happen? He speaks and he writes.

> *We proclaim to you what we have seen and heard, so that you also may have fellowship with us. And our fellowship is with the Father and with his Son, Jesus Christ. We write this to make our joy complete.*   *(1 John 1 v 3-4)*

John uses words to lead us into communion with God. And his words are Spirit-inspired words (John 16 v 13-14). God's word is given so we might experience the complete joy of communion with the triune God.

My wife was a fan of the television show *The Great British Bake Off.* Each week members of the public baked cakes, with the best bakers going through to the next round. Each episode ended with the contestants bringing their cakes to be judged. We at home could all see the cakes. Everyone in our house decided which they thought looked best. But it's not looks that count. The only real way to know whether it's a great cake is the taste test. So judge Mary Berry would put a fork of cake into her mouth, pause, smile and say, "That's lovely".

Peter invites us to apply the test taste to the Bible. "Like newborn babies," he says, "crave pure spiritual milk, so that by it you may grow up in your salvation, now that you have tasted that the Lord is good" (1 Peter 2 v 2-3). By "spiritual milk" he means "the living and enduring word of God" through which we have been born again (1 v 23). We crave the Bible because we know from experience it tastes good. But Peter doesn't say the Bible tastes good. He says "the Lord" tastes good. The point, of course, is that we taste the goodness of God in the word of God. The theologian and author Wayne Grudem comments: "In the hearing of the Lord's words believers experience the joy of personal fellowship with the Lord himself."[48]

PUTTING IT INTO PRACTICE

Since the Bible is how we hear God's voice and enjoy his presence, we'll want to be intentional about reading it. So it's great to have a Bible-reading plan or use daily Bible notes. But don't confuse the means and the end. The goal is to enjoy God, and planning to read the Bible each day is just the means. So don't feel the need to catch up if you miss a day—just skip a day or be a day behind. The goal is not ticking off a task. The aim is to hear God's voice. It's not that if you read your Bible for ten minutes, then you'll receive ten minutes' worth of grace for the day. We go to the word to hear our Saviour speak to us.

Here's a practical way of putting this into practice. Get into the habit of praying as you read the Bible. Turn God's speech into a two-way conversation by worshipping over the word. Many prayers recorded in the Bible are actually Bible promises turned round and presented back to God as requests. One way of doing this is to read the passage as a whole and then reread it a verse or two at a time. After each section, turn what you've read into prayer. You might respond with praise or confession or thanksgiving or petition. In the case of a Bible story, you might focus on two or three verses that capture your attention or summarise God's involvement.

Let's take John 14 as an example. You might read verses 1-10 to get the big picture and then re-read verse 1.

> *Do not let your hearts be troubled. You believe in God;*
> *believe also in me.* *(John 14 v 1)*

You might begin by confessing some of the ways your heart is troubled. Then rejoice in Christ's invitation to trust him. This is an opportunity to leave your troubles with him. Then re-read verses 2-3:

> *My Father's house has many rooms; if that were not so,*
> *would I have told you that I am going there to prepare a*
> *place for you? And if I go and prepare a place for you, I*
> *will come back and take you to be with me that you also*
> *may be where I am.* *(John 14 v 2-3)*

Thank Jesus for preparing a place with God for you through his death and resurrection. Thank him for the promise that he'll return so we can be with him. Ask him to help you view your troubles in the light of eternity.

[Jesus said,] "You know the way to the place where I am going." Thomas said to him, "Lord, we don't know where you are going, so how can we know the way?" Jesus answered, "I am the way and the truth and the life. No one comes to the Father except through me."   (John 14 v 4-6)

Thank Jesus for showing you the way to God and giving you the promise of eternal life. Pray that unbelieving family and friends would also come to the Father through Jesus.

[Jesus said,] "If you really know me, you will know my Father as well. From now on, you do know him and have seen him." Philip said, "Lord, show us the Father and that will be enough for us." Jesus answered: "Don't you know me, Philip, even after I have been among you such a long time? Anyone who has seen me has seen the Father."
(John 14 v 7-9)

Praise God that he has perfectly revealed himself in Jesus. Praise him for all the aspects of his character that we see in the actions and words of Jesus. Express your desire to know more of the Father by knowing more of Jesus.

How can you say, "Show us the Father"? Don't you believe that I am in the Father, and that the Father is in me? The words I say to you I do not speak on my own authority. Rather, it is the Father, living in me, who is doing his work.   (John 14 v 9-10)

Through the words that Jesus speaks (written for us in the Bible), the Father does his work. We're back where we started. God is present and active through his word. Pray that God will be at work through the words of Jesus in your life, in your church and in the mission of your church.

Reading the Bible is an *educational* process. We learn about God as we read. But it's much, much more than this. It's also a *relational* process. Every word we read or hear preached is an opportunity to enjoy communion with God. In every word we can meet God and hear his voice.

Why do I say to my wife, "I love you"? After all, I've told her before. It's not new information. Yet she never complains when I tell her again. The words "I love you" reassure her and enable her to feel secure. It's the same with God's people, whom Jesus speaks of as his bride. Every day our sin gives us reasons to wonder whether Christ still loves us. But every day—if we will only listen—Christ reassures us of his love in his word. Your primary aim as you read the Bible is not to seek out new or novel ideas (although you may meet some new ideas as you read). Make it your aim to hear God's voice and meet him in his word.

ACTION

Each day this week pray through a passage of Scripture.

MIKE AND EMMA'S MONDAY MORNING

Mike closes his eyes. He tries to recall yesterday's sermon. What had his pastor said? Something about Christ being our righteousness. Nothing new. Mike had heard it many times before. But it was such a comfort to hear again yesterday. And it is a comfort to remember it again this morning.

Mike thinks of the day ahead. It's so easy for him to find identity in his work. If the day has gone well, he will feel great about himself. But when it goes badly, he will trudge home in a despondent mood. His mind goes to this afternoon's monthly review meeting with his boss. How will he feel after that? But then he thinks of himself standing before God, clothed with the righteousness of Christ. He thinks of all Christ's worth being wrapped around him,

Mike. During yesterday's sermon it had felt as if God was speaking directly to him. A word from God just for him, just for this afternoon's meeting. "And now," he thinks, "the Holy Spirit is reminding me of that word".

Meanwhile, and a little late, Emma's walking up the path to Amanda's front door. They meet most weeks to read the Bible together and pray. Emma tries to remember what it was they looked at last week. Something in Philippians. Something about knowing Christ. Whatever it was, she remembers feeling excited about it at the time.

That's right: to live is Christ and to die is gain—something like that. The Holy Spirit had really spoken to her as she and Amanda had read together. Even death is good news if you're living for Christ. It had been so reassuring. It still is. No matter what might happen to her or her family she'll always have Christ. "I need to keep hearing that," Emma thinks. "Thank you, Holy Spirit, for reminding me of the gospel last week. Please keep it fresh in my mind."

REFLECTION QUESTIONS

- The previous chapter ended with a challenge to spend time thinking about eternal life in the new creation. How have you got on? What difference has this made?
- When does reading the Bible feel like a wonderful delight to you? When does it feel like a wearying duty? What makes the difference?
- When was the last time you felt God speaking to you through his word? How could you approach his word to listen for his voice?
- How do you plan your Bible-reading? What changes might you make?
- How have you experienced the Holy Spirit's involvement in your life over the last 24 hours?

IN ONE ANOTHER WE CAN ENJOY GOD'S LOVE

G od has given us the church to help us enjoy him. The Christian community is the main context where you experience divine joy. I realise that's a bold claim. Look round the room next time you meet with your church and it might not look very promising. But if you look with the eyes of faith, you'll see in your brothers and sisters a hundred ways in which divine joy and love are made complete.

DIVINE JOY IS MADE COMPLETE IN THE CHRISTIAN COMMUNITY

John opens his first letter with an invitation to enjoy God: "We proclaim to you what we have seen and heard, so that you also may have fellowship with us. And our fellowship is with the Father and with his Son, Jesus Christ. We write this to make our joy complete" (1 John 1 v 3-4). What's John's recipe? Here are the ingredients. First, start with the proclamation of the Word of life (1 v 1-2). Second, throw in fellowship with Christians, who are connected to the first apostles by what those apostles wrote in the New Testament (1 v 3-4). Leave it to simmer for a while and the result is complete joy. Word, community and joy all mingle together. We experience joy as the Bible is read and proclaimed in the Christian community.

The German theologian and martyr Dietrich Bonhoeffer said, "The Christ in [our] own hearts is weaker than the Christ in the word of other Christians."[49] Here's what he means. There are often moments when our hearts condemn us (1 John 3 v 19-22). Perhaps we've fallen into sin; perhaps we're plagued by doubt. Our minds are in a stew and our hearts are muddled. Then another Christian speaks. It might be the preacher on a Sunday morning. It might be in a conversation with a friend. The point is those words come to you from outside. This is not your internal monologue with all its confusions. These words come as an objective declaration of good news to your heart.

This is our experience. Most of the moments in which we've felt God speaking have come through other Christians. Of course, it can happen while you're reading the Bible on your own. But more often it happens through others. We find the same dynamic in prayer. We struggle to pray for extended periods on our own, but in a prayer meeting we somehow energise one another.

Bonhoeffer linked this to the idea that what makes us righteous comes from outside of us. We're not made right with God because of anything *within* us—it's not that we get ourselves good enough for God. Instead, what makes us right with God is the righteousness of Jesus. It comes from *outside* of us. Bonhoeffer said:

> *In themselves [Christians] are destitute and dead. Help must come from the outside; and it has come and comes daily and anew in the Word of Jesus Christ ... But God put his Word into the mouth of human beings so that it may be passed on to others ... Therefore, Christians need*

*other Christians who speak God's Word to them. They
need them again and again when they become uncertain and
disheartened because, living by their own resources, they
cannot help themselves.*[50]

You don't need the Christian community to know that
you're forgiven by God—but it helps! Sometimes our hearts
condemn us and the word of Christ spoken by a brother or
sister cuts through the confusion.

In the film *The Mission*, set in eighteenth-century Latin
America, the repentant slave-trader Mendoza (played by
Robert De Niro) climbs a waterfall as an act of penance,
with his armour—the symbol of his past life—roped to
his back. The film powerfully portrays his struggle to reach
the top. Release only comes when one of the indigenous
people, whom he had formerly terrorised, cuts the rope so
that his burden falls away. The objective reality of acceptance with God becomes a liberating experience through
the acceptance of others.

Our sung worship is a particular opportunity to recapture
joy in God together. As we sing, we declare truth. But we
declare it with music, so it appeals to our emotions. Not only
that, but we engage our whole bodies in the act: we stand, fill
our lungs and perhaps lift our hands. And we sing together.
It's a communal act which conveys a strong sense of solidar-
ity. I'm not alone. We together as God's people are enjoying
God's grace. Time and again, the truth we know in our heads
captivates our hearts through worship. Body and soul, words
and music, you and I—all combine to give us joy in God.

DIVINE LOVE IS MADE COMPLETE IN THE CHRISTIAN COMMUNITY

John continues, "We know that we have come to know
him if we keep his commands" (1 John 2 v 3). John has a

specific command in mind here. In verses 1 John 2 v 7-8 he talks about an old command that is a new command. What's that all about? John has in mind the words of Jesus: "A new command I give you: love one another. As I have loved you, so you must love one another" (John 13 v 34). It's the old command to love, but Jesus has given it a new twist. We're to love like Jesus. So for John, obeying the commands of Jesus is another way of saying, *Love like Jesus.*

John lists three false claims (1 John 2 v 4, 6, 9). They're the claims of people who say they know God but don't love their Christian brothers and sisters. For example, "Whoever says, 'I know him,' but does not do what he commands"—that is, his command to love the Christian community—"is a liar, and the truth is not in that person" (2 v 4). That's the negative. But again with each false claim John gives a positive encouragement: "But if anyone obeys his word"—to love the Christian community—"love for God is truly made complete in them" (2 v 5).

Back in 1 John 1 v 4, *divine joy is made complete* in the Christian community as it proclaims the word of Christ. Now *divine love is made complete* in the Christian community as we love one another. Love for God becomes complete love when we love our brothers and sisters. Or God's love for us reaches its true goal when we love one another. You can't enjoy God's love on your own.

So you can't love God on your own! Love for God only becomes complete when you love other people. You've got to be part of a Christian community. That's what it means to know Jesus, obey Jesus and live like Jesus (1 John 2 v 3-6).

WE ENJOY GOD WHEN WE *RECEIVE* LOVE

"No one has ever seen God; but if we love one another," says John in 1 John 4 v 12-13, "God lives in us and his love is made *complete* in us". John's point is this: we can't see

God, but we can see one another. So we *see* the love of the invisible God in the love of the visible church. God's love becomes a reality that can be seen and heard and touched in the life of the Christian community.

And brotherly love isn't a poor substitute for the real thing. For brotherly love *is* divine love. God loves us *through* the love of other Christians. He loves us in other ways, of course—supremely in the gift of his Son. But the love we experience from other Christians starts with God.

The brother who speaks a word of comfort to you, the sister who bakes a cake for you, the family who welcome you into their home—all are the hands and feet of God. When a brother hugs you, Christ is hugging you. When a sister sits by your hospital bed, Christ is sitting by your bedside. When a friend weeps with you, Christ is weeping with you.

Christian love is the overflow of God's love to us. "Dear friends, let us love one another, for love comes from God ... Dear friends, since God so loved us, we also ought to love one another" (1 John 4 v 7, 11). God's love is poured into me through Jesus, and some of that love spills over to my brothers and sisters. It's certainly not generated within me; it comes from God.

WE ENJOY GOD WHEN WE *GIVE* LOVE

"For what is our hope, our joy, or the crown in which we will glory in the presence of our Lord Jesus when he comes?" That's the question Paul asks in 1 Thessalonians 2 v 19-20. How would you answer? Here's Paul's answer: "Is it not you? Indeed, you are our glory and joy." He says much the same thing to the church in Philippi. He speaks of them as "you whom I love and long for, my joy and crown" (Philippians 4 v 1). What's your pride and joy? Paul's pride and joy was the churches to whom he was connected.

John says something similar at the beginning of 1 John. "We write this," he says in 1 v 4, "to make *our* joy complete". You might have expected him to say, "to make *your* joy complete". After all, it's clear he writes to bring his readers joy. So why say "*our* joy"? Because for John "your joy" *is* "our joy". What John enjoys is seeing other Christians experience joy. There's nothing he likes more than people rejoicing in Christ. That's *complete* joy.

Pursuing my joy in Christ can be self-defeating. If it's a self-centred exercise in self-fulfilment, then joy will elude you—even joy in Christ. But if we pursue *one another's* joy, then our joy and love are made complete. So if you want to find joy, you may need to stop looking for joy and instead start working for the joy of others. The strange fact is that you'll never really be happy while you're pursuing your own happiness.

Recently my wife said, "You're weary, you sigh when people ask you to do things and you're not being intentional in discipleship". Wham! She was right though. Everything I had to do felt like a burden. I was trying to do what would make me happy, but it wasn't working. Her words flicked a switch. Nothing changed and everything changed. Tasks that had felt like a burden became a joy as I tried to reorient myself towards others.

To give is to gain in the economy of Christ. I don't mean this in the sense touted by the "prosperity gospel". I'm not suggesting that giving money will lead to a full bank account. That lie suggests you give up earthly treasures to gain more earthly treasures. It actually reinforces the selfishness that robs us of true joy.

But it is true that we find ourselves by giving ourselves. Our problem is that too often we want to be radical Christians leading comfortable lives. We want to *give everything* for Christ and to *have everything* this life offers. We want to tell the world about Christ and we want to be liked by our peers. We want to grow more like Jesus and enjoy the pleasures of this world. But this double-mindedness doesn't work. Pleasure-seekers soon become world-weary. High achievers are insecure. Jesus said:

> *Whoever wants to be my disciple must deny themselves and take up their cross and follow me. For whoever wants to save their life will lose it, but whoever loses their life for me and for the gospel will save it. What good is it for someone to gain the whole world, yet forfeit their soul?*
>
> *(Mark 8 v 34-36)*

To gain a life that is rich and full—a life into which eternity has begun to shine—we need to lose ourselves and show the sacrificial love of the cross.

Try this thought experiment with me. Think about the Christians you know who are most preoccupied with their own needs and desires. And think about the Christians you know who are unhappy. I suspect you'll find a big overlap. Now list the Christians you know who think about others the most. I suspect you'll find they're among the happiest Christians you know. It's counter-intuitive, but the more you deny yourself to love others, the more joy you experience.

By all means hang out with people your age or who share your interests. But what's distinctive about Christ-like love is the way it crosses ethnic, generational and social divides. So love the people in your church. Don't just serve them as some kind of duty. Enjoy them. Spend time with them. Build community with them. Loving your Christian community will bring deep and lasting rewards.

John says an amazing thing in 1 John 2 v 8 that's easy to miss. He says, "I am writing you a new command; its truth is seen in him *and in you*". The distinctive character of

Christian love that's seen in Jesus is also seen *in you.* Your church may have all sorts of problems and failings. It may seem very ordinary. But see beyond that for a moment. Look at your community as John sees it. He sees the light of the new age taking shape in your community (2 v 9-11). We're the prototype of the new creation. The future has broken into history and can be seen in your Christian community. Our cities and towns are places in spiritual darkness. But every time a new church is started, it's as if God switches on a light. Light shines through Christian love.

There are two men in my church who often speak fondly of the time when they worked together to renovate the home one of them had just bought. It's often like that with men. We don't share our emotions face to face. Instead, we bond best when we're alongside one another—walking, working, playing, serving. It's the same with Jesus. We feel closest to Jesus when we're serving alongside him. In the topsy-turvy world of the kingdom of God:

- we find ourselves by losing ourselves.
- we gain most when we give most.
- we experience fulfilment when we deny ourselves.
- we feel happy most when we pursue the happiness of others.

PUTTING IT INTO PRACTICE

How can your Christian community help you enjoy God? How can you help others enjoy God? Here are some ideas.

1. *Find someone to pray with one to one.* You don't have to tell everyone about your struggles, but having at least one person with whom you're honest and open makes a massive difference. Find someone who'll love you enough to tell it straight—someone who will "speak the truth in love" (Ephesians 4 v 15). Hear

their words as a message from Christ himself. And don't forget to speak the truth in love to them as well.

2. *Let people sing to you.* One of the things I like to do from time to time is to stop singing and listen as if the song is being sung just for me. It can be a very powerful moment. All the truth of the song is directed with all the power of the music to my heart. Wham! Of course, we can't all do it at the same time; otherwise no one would be left singing. But give it a go from time to time. It helps if you sit near the front so most people are singing in your direction—a wall of sound coming your way to stir your emotions.

3. *Look at people when you take communion.* People often make the Lord's Supper a private moment between me and God. But it's a communal act. "Because there is one loaf, we, who are many, are one body, for we all share the one loaf" (1 Corinthians 10 v 17). So look at your brothers and sisters taking the bread and wine. Reflect on God's grace in their lives. Think what a beautiful thing it is that these diverse people come together as family through the gospel.

4. *Invite someone for a meal.* Jesus spent much of his ministry at a meal table with people. This is how he expressed community with people and this is how he did mission. By eating with sinners, he powerfully embodied God's grace to them. And we, too, can embody grace to people round a meal table. It's a way to offer friendship. If your circumstances make hosting people difficult, then invite people out for a drink or a picnic. A meal is the best first step towards living in community.[51]

ACTION
Initiate a meal with someone from your church.

MIKE AND EMMA'S MONDAY MORNING
"Sorry about the mess," says Amanda. Emma smiles. It's always messy in Amanda's house. She moves a pile of laundry off the chair onto the table so she can sit down. Amanda hands her a rather strong cup of tea. Emma doesn't know how Amanda copes with the chaos.

But she wouldn't skip their weekly time together, not for the world. Amanda has been such an encouragement over the past few years. It's so helpful to talk things through, pray together, share a few tears. When Rosie died, there were times when Emma questioned God's love. But somehow God's love always felt more certain after she'd spent time with Amanda.

"You are literally a God-send," says Emma. Amanda raises a questioning eyebrow. "It's not been a good start to the day," explains Emma. "But here you are with a cup of tea—a little gift from God." "Me or the tea? Which is the gift from God?" Emma smiles. "Both. Definitely both."

REFLECTION QUESTIONS
- The previous chapter ended with a challenge to pray through the Scriptures. How have you got on?
- When has a word from another Christian had a powerful impact on your heart, or when have you experienced the love of God through the kindness of other Christians?
- When have you found the selfish pursuit of happiness to be self-defeating?

- Think about the Christians you know who are most preoccupied with themselves, their desires and their status. And then think about the Christians you know who are most preoccupied with serving others and with God's glory. Who are the happiest?
- To give is to gain in the economy of Christ. What could you give?

IN DAILY REPENTANCE AND FAITH WE CAN ENJOY GOD'S FREEDOM

Think about human relationships. Think what happens when you let someone down. How do you then relate to them? I can't speak for you, but I don't look forward to seeing them. I'm embarrassed and ashamed. I worry about how they'll treat me. If I can, I'll often opt to avoid them.

Or maybe you've had the opposite experience—the experience of reconciliation. A relationship went bad and you felt the pain of that break. Then finally you swallowed your pride and said, "Sorry". And the person forgave you and the relationship was restored. Often that brings a feeling of elation—all that was lost has been regained.

Our relationship with God works along similar lines. When we let God down by sinning, then the relationship feels broken. It isn't broken—God still loves us. That's a vital truth to remember. But it *feels* broken to us. We feel ashamed and we may opt to keep our distance. The wonderful truth is that when we turn back to God in repentance, then joy in God returns.

As I've reflected on what it means to enjoy God, I think this is the number one reason I don't enjoy God more than I do: not enough repentance.

The problem is *not* that I sin. Sin itself doesn't keep us from God because God is gracious and he has provided a means of reconciliation through the work of his Son. So sin itself doesn't prevent us enjoying God. The problem is either:

- I keep my distance from God because I'm choosing sin over God, *or*
- I keep my distance from God because I feel ashamed.

And the solution in both cases is repentance.

Repentance doesn't sound like fun. It involves admitting you're wrong or saying no to the pleasures of sin. But think of repentance as the gateway to the pleasures of God. It can be a squeeze sometimes passing through the gate. But on the other side is a wide open space, filled with light and love.

THE SECRET OF HAPPINESS

In Psalm 32 David invites us to follow him through the gate of repentance into the pleasure park of God's love. He begins with some wisdom:

> *¹ Blessed is the one*
> *whose transgressions are forgiven,*
> *whose sins are covered.*
> *² Blessed is the one*
> *whose sin the* LORD *does not count against them*
> *and in whose spirit is no deceit.* (Psalm 32 v 1-2)

Here's the secret of happiness. Who is the blessed or happy one? *Not* the person who is free from sin. Such a person doesn't exist. "Blessed is the one who does not sin" wouldn't be good news. It would only crush us. Of course, we call one another to obedience. But the good news of this psalm is that you don't have to wait until you achieve some higher level of godliness before you can enjoy God's blessing. Enjoying God is *never* something we achieve. It's his gift to us in Christ. A blessed life is open to you *now*. The secret is not perfection, but forgiveness.

We have three expressions for this reconciliation in verses 1-2. First, our sins are "forgiven" (Psalm 32 v 1). That is, they are taken away. Psalm 103 v 12 says, "As far as the east is from the west, so far has he removed our transgressions from us". It's a wonderful image because east and west just keep on going further away from each other. In the Old Testament on the Day of Atonement, two goats were chosen. One was sacrificed as a substitute for the penalty of sin. The other had the sins of the people confessed on its head before being driven from the camp (Leviticus 16 v 8-10). It was a powerful picture of our sin being carried away so that it disappears over the horizon.

Second, our sins are "covered" (Psalm 32 v 1). After Adam and Eve rebelled against God, they realised they were naked and they felt ashamed. So they hid from God. And that's my experience. I sin—and then I hide from God. I keep my distance. I'm always hesitant to pray that first prayer after I've sinned. But God made clothes of animal skins for Adam and Eve (Genesis 3 v 21). It was a picture of the sacrifice of his Son, which covers our shame. We can come before God—even when we've sinned—with confidence because we're clothed in the righteousness of his Son.

Third, the LORD does not count our sin against us (Psalm 32 v 2). These verses are quoted by Paul in Romans 4 v 6-8. Paul's point is that through faith God no longer counts our sins against us and instead he counts us right in Christ. Our sins are credited to Christ and he bears them on the cross. And instead Christ's righteousness is credited to us.

This is the experience of anyone who turns to God in repentance. So what's the problem? Why don't we experience more of this happiness?

UNCONFESSED SIN RUINS OUR ENJOYMENT OF GOD

This is how David describes his own experience of lost joy.

> *³ When I kept silent,*
>   *my bones wasted away*
>   *through my groaning all day long.*
> *⁴ For day and night*
>   *your hand was heavy on me;*
> *my strength was sapped*
>   *as in the heat of summer.* (Psalm 32 v 3-4)

His loss of joy is all wrapped in the words "I kept silent" (v 3). David refused to acknowledge his sin and instead covered it up (as the contrast with v 5 makes clear). He bluffed it out. He brushed it under the carpet.

You can be an expert at hiding your sin from other people. But it doesn't bring joy. You think exposure will be a disaster. But covering up doesn't make you happy. Instead we're left with a deep feeling of unease. By delaying repentance, we step away from the love and life of God. Our unease may even take bodily form. David feels it in his bones. Today we talk about psychosomatic problems. But readers of the Bible have always known that our mental state can affect our physical wellbeing.

God is not passive in this situation. He doesn't leave us, as it were, hiding in the cold. He pursues us in his love. "Day and night your hand was heavy on me," says David (v 4). Sometimes God increases our pain, but his aim is always to lead us back to greater joy. Your unhappiness may be God's call to find happiness in him.

Most of us, I suspect, are willing to acknowledge that we're sinners in a general sense. We join in our church's prayers of confession each Sunday. So what's the problem? Perhaps the key is the word "deceit" in verse 2. Verse 2 says blessed are those "in whose spirit is no deceit". Verses 3-4 describe those in whose spirit there is deceit. Here are three "tactics" we use to avoid true repentance.

1. *We minimise sin.* David doesn't say the problem is guilty *feelings*. The problem is guilt. It's an objective reality. He speaks in verse 5 of "the guilt of my sin". My sin is wrong. And it's not a small thing. It's not a slip-up. It's an attempt to dethrone God.

2. *We excuse sin.* "I've done the wrong thing," we say, "but..." We plead mitigating circumstances. "I was under so much pressure... The temptation was overwhelming..." We blame our hormones or our family history or our circumstances. It's God's fault really, we argue, for letting this situation arise.

3. *We indulge temptation.* The Bible tells us to *flee* temptation (1 Timothy 6 v 11). Whenever you see temptation, you're supposed to run in the opposite direction. But this is what I do. I don't say yes to temptation, but I don't say no either. I indulge the thought. I delay any decisive rejection. I hedge my bets. And it's very hard to come before God in prayer when you're entertaining a rejection of him!

There are good reasons why we can't minimise or excuse our sin or indulge temptation—reasons why it's theologically inconsistent. But let's stick with the reason given in this psalm: it leads to misery. Your heart will groan (v 3) and your energy will be sapped (v 4). And that's because it's keeping you from enjoying God: it keeps you from his life, power and love.

CONFESSING SIN RESTORES OUR ENJOYMENT OF GOD

The only true and lasting solution is to acknowledge and confess your sin.

> *Then I acknowledged my sin to you*
> *and did not cover up my iniquity.*
> *I said, "I will confess*
> *my transgressions to the LORD."*
> *And you forgave*
> *the guilt of my sin.*   *(Psalm 32 v 5)*

The striking thing about this verse is there's no gap between confession and forgiveness. No delay. No requirements. As soon as David confessed his sin, he was forgiven by God.

You can make David's experience of renewed joy in God *your* experience of renewed joy. You may have been groaning under the weight of hidden sin or have indulged temptation for years. And today it can be forgiven. It can be wiped away, as it were, in the space of a single verse. One act of true confession is all that's required. David turns his own experience into an invitation for all God's people.

> *⁶ Therefore let all the faithful pray to you*
> *while you may be found;*
> *surely the rising of the mighty waters*
> *will not reach them.*
> *⁷ You are my hiding-place;*
> *you will protect me from trouble*
> *and surround me with songs of deliverance.*
>   *(Psalm 32 v 6-7)*

David speaks of being safe from "mighty waters" (v 6). It reminds us of Noah's flood, where the water represents

God's judgment (Genesis 6 – 9). We meet the same imagery again in Exodus 14 when the people of Israel passed through the Red Sea to safety while the Egyptian army was judged by mighty waters. As a result, the Israelites sang a song of deliverance in Exodus 15—just as David does in verse 7. By confessing sin and receiving forgiveness, we're participating in the bigger story of God's people. You can experience what Noah experienced when he escaped the flood, and what the Israelites experienced when they passed through the Red Sea, and what all God's people experienced when we died and rose again in Christ. We pass through God's judgment in Christ and enter the kingdom of his love.

Let's suppose you've had a row with your husband or wife. You've shouted at them. Stormed out the house. Slammed the door. As you set off for work, you replay the conversation with ever more effective put-downs. But, as the emotions subside, you realise it was partly your fault. Partly? OK, mainly. You were selfish, proud and self-righteous. So how are you feeling now? Your spouse has a good track record of forgiving you, but still you wonder whether they'll vent their frustration or give you the cold shoulder. And so you head home at the end of the day with a degree of reluctance. You hope they'll have forgotten about it, though that seems unlikely. As you walk through the door, you shout a cheerful greeting, but you can't look them in the eye. There's a bit a small talk, but you can feel the tension underneath. You're tempted to bluff it out—ignore the elephant in the room until it goes away. But this is miserable. There's only one solution. "I'm so sorry about what I said this morning." What happens next? More often than not, there's forgiveness followed by a renewed affection for one another.

Here's how it works with me and God. I've sinned against him in a way that weighs heavily on my mind. I know he's gracious and I know Christ has died for my sin, including this particular sin. But I'm reluctant to pray. I keep my distance from God, as it were. I feel ashamed. The result? Misery. So eventually I sink my pride, overcome my fear and turn back to God. "Sorry, Father. What I did was wrong. There are no excuses. It was an act of ungrateful disobedience. Please forgive me. Remember your promises, your mercy, the shed blood of Jesus." Result? Renewed joy, often with a fresh sense of God's amazing grace.

AN INVITATION TO ENJOY GOD

Don't be as stubborn as a mule. That's David's exhortation in verse 9:

> *Do not be like the horse or the mule,*
>   *which have no understanding*
> *but must be controlled by bit and bridle*
>   *or they will not come to you.*   *(Psalm 32 v 9)*

Don't be too proud to admit your failure. Don't be too ashamed to expose your guilt. Don't keep your distance. Instead, be wise and come to God willingly, freely, joyfully.

God doesn't keep you at arm's length when you sin. He's not keeping his distance until you've suffered enough and atoned for your sin. Christ has already paid the price of your sin in full—including the specific sin that you're currently thinking about. It's taken away and covered over (v 1).

If God feels distant, it's because *you* are holding *him* at arm's length. Perhaps you nurture temptation so that your heart is divided. Perhaps you're hiding in shame. There's no need. God is ready to surround you with his unfailing love. Listen to the words of Jesus to the church of Laodicea:

> *Those whom I love I rebuke and discipline. So be earnest*
> *and repent. Here I am! I stand at the door and knock. If*
> *anyone hears my voice and opens the door, I will come in*
> *and eat with that person, and they with me.*
>
> *(Revelation 3 v 19-20)*

This is often used as an invitation to unbelievers to "let Jesus into your heart". But it's actually spoken to believers. Jesus is there, knocking at the door. He wants to come in and eat with you. In other words, he wants you to enjoy a relationship with him. Don't hold him at arm's length.

Let me give you four suggestions for what ongoing repentance might look like. Let's call them "the disciplines of repentance".

1. *Repent of every sin.* When you sin, say "sorry" to God right away. Don't leave it. Deal with it right away. And in that act make sure you also reject the sin—don't hold on to any thought of maybe enjoying that same sin in the future.

2. *Repent from every temptation.* Temptation is not sin. Hebrews says Jesus was tempted yet without sin (Hebrews 4 v 15). But we are to flee temptation. The word "repentance" means "turning". It means turning from sin to God. But it can also involve turning from temptation to God. We're to say a decisive "No" when we feel sin calling. So let me encourage you actively to reject sin whenever you feel tempted. In that moment say no to sin and yes to Jesus. Say it aloud if you can do so without embarrassment. Pray a quick prayer. And then turn round and run in the opposite direction. Flee temptation.

3. *Repent every day.* Have a regular moment each day when you think back over the last 24 hours and repent of any sin of which you're aware. The easiest thing to do would be to make this part of your daily Bible-reading and prayer. Ask the Spirit to reveal your sin. The aim is not to make you feel bad about yourself. Quite the opposite. The aim is to replace the groaning of verses 3-4 with the happiness of verses 1-2.

4. *Repent every week.* If your church has a prayer of confession, either in its liturgy or led from the front, treasure that moment and put it to good use. I usually pray on my walk to my office. I start by confessing my sin as I walk down our road. And then I turn the corner and walk up the hill through the trees. And that's the moment I begin to look forward to our time of corporate confession during next Sunday morning's service. I know God has forgiven me. But I still enjoy hearing his word of assurance and forgiveness in the Christian community.

What happens next all depends on your view of God. You can choose the pleasures of sin or the pleasures of God. You can hide in fear or come to God in confession. What choice you make all turns on how you view God. The American author A. W. Tozer said, "Were we able to extract from any man a complete answer to the question, 'What comes into your mind when you think about God?' we might predict with certainty the spiritual future of that man."[52]

The key phrase in this psalm is in verse 10: "The LORD's unfailing love surrounds the one who trusts in him". You will not turn to God unless you think his love is unfailing and that you are surrounded by it. This psalm invites us to be wrapped around by the Father's love.

If you view God as a harsh judge or a cruel king, then you'll keep your distance. Of course you will. In the Garden of Eden, Satan portrayed God as a tyrant—and humanity has been hiding from God ever since.

But Jesus reveals God as a loving Father. We're back where we started, with the Trinity. Jesus the Son of God enables us to share his experience of sonship. The Father loves those who are in Son with the same love that he has towards his Son. John Calvin says, "No one gives himself freely and willingly to God's service unless, having tasted his fatherly love, he is drawn to love and worship him in return."[53]

What's the reason God loves you? Our instinct is often to look within for an answer. In our pride we want to think that in some way we deserve God's love. But when we look within what we find is sin. Looking within leads to deep insecurity because inside we're ugly. We find reasons for God *not* to love us. So look instead to Christ and the cross. For "God demonstrates his own love for us in this: while we were still sinners, Christ died for us" (Romans 5 v 8).

Here's the conclusion: "Rejoice in the LORD and be glad, you righteous; sing, all you who are upright in heart!" (Psalm 32 v 11). The psalm ends with three commands: "Rejoice ... be glad ... sing". Those are happy commands! Charles Wesley wrote a hymn based on this psalm entitled, "Jesus, lover of my soul, let me to thy bosom fly". It ends:

Plenteous grace with thee is found,
Grace to cover all my sin.
Let the healing streams abound;
Make and keep me pure within.
Thou of life the fountain art,
Freely let me take of thee;
Spring thou up within my heart;
Rise to all eternity.

PUTTING IT INTO PRACTICE

Each day this week spend time identifying, confessing and rejecting sin. Ask yourself four questions:

1. *What excuses am I making?* Lots of us hate the effects of sin in our lives—the sense of shame or the broken relationships. But we still love the sin itself. So we blame our upbringing or other people or our circumstances. It allows us to leave our sin untouched. But if you're not murdering sin, then sin will be murdering you.

2. *How can I flee temptation?* Don't ask, "What am I allowed to do?" or "What can I get away with?" Ask yourself, "How far can I run?" How can you avoid things that encourage you to think in a wrong way? How can you avoid situations where you might be tempted?

3. *How can I embrace God instead?* How does God offer more than your sin? How can you stir your affections so your love for Jesus is bigger than your love for sin?

4. *Who can help me?* Who could you ask to encourage you, challenge you and hold you accountable? Who will tell it straight? Don't just look for sympathy. A little sympathy is a good thing, but indiscriminate sympathy encourages you in your discontent or victimhood. Who will point you away from your excuses and towards Jesus?

ACTION

Each day this week spend time identifying, confessing and rejecting sin.

MIKE AND EMMA'S MONDAY MORNING

Half an hour late, Mike is finally sitting at his desk. "How was church?" Bob had asked. Bob is Mike's only Christian colleague. How was church? The truth is it seems a long time ago. Yesterday his pastor had spoken of a relationship with God. And on Sunday it had seemed like a real possibility. But that was Sunday and this is Monday. Today it feels so much more elusive. If only he had more time to pray, then maybe he could enjoy God. Maybe he could recreate that feeling he had enjoyed on Sunday morning. Or maybe he will just have to wait until next Sunday. Next Sunday? It is still only Monday morning.

But Mike thinks again. God has had his fingerprints all over Mike's Monday morning. Mike thinks of that bacon sandwich—a gift from his Father. He thinks of the Father's purpose in the train delays (even if that was a bit mysterious) and his delight in Mike's faltering prayers. He thinks of the Son's grace in Mike's failures, his presence in his grief, his touch at communion. He thinks of the Spirit's help in temptation, his reminder of coming glory and the way he has spoken through God's word. Even Bob is a sign of God's love. It has been a busy morning for God!

"Father, you're so involved in my life every day. Forgive me for all the times I've avoided you because I want to live my life my way. I fail so often. But your love is unfailing. I want to live my life surrounded by that unfailing love."

REFLECTION QUESTIONS
- The previous chapter ended with a challenge to initiate a meal with someone from your church. How have you got on?
- What are some of the ways you minimise sin, excuse sin or indulge temptation?

- What are your "rhythms" of repentance? Is there something you need to do to build it into your routine?
- Whether you turn to God in repentance depends on how you view him. Think back to the last time you felt guilty for sin. How did you view God? How does Psalm 32 v 10 teach us to view God in these moments?
- Think of a specific sin with which you struggle. Ask yourself: What excuses am I making? How can I flee temptation? How can I embrace God instead? Who can help me?

UNDER
THE HOOD

Y ou don't need to know how an engine works to be able to drive a car. And you don't need to know the theological underpinning of this book to enjoy a relationship with God. But knowing something about how an engine works can help, especially when something goes wrong.

There are two principles underlying this book—the principle of three and one, and the principle of union and communion.

- They have the capacity to transform our relationship with God.
- They are very simple, requiring no special skills.
- They are not often talked about today.

But they're not new. I would love to be able to claim the credit for them, but in fact they're derived from *Communion with God*, a book written in 1657 by the great Puritan theologian John Owen.[54] The full title of the book is: *Of Communion with God the Father, Son and Holy Ghost, Each Person Distinctly, in Love, Grace, and Consolation; or the Saints' Fellowship with the Father, Son and Holy Ghost Unfolded.* It's not very

snappy, but it does introduce us to our first foundational principle: *God is known through the three Persons, so we relate to the Father, the Son and the Spirit.*

1. THE PRINCIPLE OF THREE AND ONE

Christian theology has always said God's essence or nature is unknowable. We can only make negative statements about God: God is *un*changing, *im*movable, *in*finite and so on. Any description of God's nature would involve categories and concepts beyond our comprehension. So we can only say what his nature is *not* like. Even apparently positive statements about God's nature should really be seen as negative statements. To say that God is spirit, for example, is only really saying that he doesn't have a body. We can't analyse the chemical composition of God's spirit or sequence its DNA. So we can't relate to the nature of God because his nature is unknowable.

Nevertheless we can know God because God is known in and through the *Persons* of God. The God who is three Persons in relationship enters into a relationship with us. A force or an idea can't have a two-way relationship. But God is not some impersonal force that flows through the universe, nor a set of moral principles that earlier generations thought of as a person. He's not even *love writ large* in some abstract sense. We're not trying to relate to a "thing", an "it" or a "force". Who wants to pray to a thing?

Instead God is three Persons. He's always been three Persons, living in community with one another. So God has always had the capacity for relationship with others because the Persons of God have always existed in relationship with each other. So, while we don't have a relationship with the essence of God, we do have a relationship with the Father, with the Son and with the Spirit.

Owen says:

> *The saints have distinct communion with the Father, and*
> *the Son, and the Holy Spirit (that is, distinctly with the*
> *Father, and distinctly with the Son, and distinctly with the*
> *Holy Spirit).*[55]

We're not interacting with abstract ideas. We're engaging with persons. The nearest models we have of how we relate to the triune God is as a child relates to his Father, a sister to her brother, a wife to her husband, a friend to his friend. John Calvin puts it like this:

> *The Scriptural teaching concerning God's infinite and*
> *spiritual essence ought to be enough, not only to banish*
> *popular delusions, but also to refute the subtleties of*
> *secular philosophy.*[56]

In other words, what the Bible tells us about God's essence only really tells us how *little* we can understand of God. But just when you might be about to despair of any real knowledge of God, Calvin continues by saying that God offers himself "to be contemplated clearly in three Persons. Unless we grasp these, only the base and empty name of God flits about in our brains, to the exclusion of the true God."[57] In other words, without an encounter with the three Persons, the word "God" has no content for us. We could use the word, but the only meaning we could give it would come from our own imagination. It would never bear any relation to the true essence of God. But in the Persons of God, we have a true encounter with the true God.

Think of it like this. We might ask, "How can you know what it's like to be a dog?" The answer is you can't. You can never experience the essence or being of dog-ness. But you can know specific dogs. You can have a very intimate relationship with Rover, your pet pooch. It's the same with

God—only much more so. We can't know what it's like to
be a dog, but both humans and dogs are mammals, so we do
have some common experiences. We assume we feel hunger
and warmth in similar ways. If your dog falls in a cold river
(as mine often did) and crawls out looking bedraggled and
cold, you have some sense of what he's experiencing. But
God is a completely different being to us. His experience of
"Godness" is totally beyond our comprehension. There's no
way we can even have vague parallels to the essence of God.

But we can know the Persons of God. Owen says:

> *There is no grace whereby our souls go forth to God, no
> act of divine worship yielded to him, no duty or obedience
> performed, which is not distinctly related to Father, Son,
> and Spirit.*[58]

In other words, we always relate to God by relating to the
persons of God. This is the way, concludes Owen, that "we
have communion with God ... we have that communion
distinctly" with each of the three Persons.[59]

It's a simple idea that, as we've seen, is actually quite easy
to apply. As you think about relating to God, think about
how you relate to each member of the Trinity distinctly.
Think about how the Father is acting towards you, how
the Son is acting towards you and how the Spirit is acting
towards you. And then, in each case, think about how you
might respond.

When you pray, for example, think of addressing your
words to the Father through the Son with the help of the
Spirit. Or when you read the Bible, think of the Father revealing himself in his Son by the Holy Spirit or think of the
Son communicating his love to you through the Holy Spirit.

Alongside a recognition that God is three Persons, we
must always hold the recognition that God is one Being.

We must also never separate the three Persons from the one Being. Christians don't believe in three gods.

This means the work of one is the work of all three—and to experience one is to experience all three. In John 14, Jesus says that an encounter with him is an encounter with God:

- *To know Jesus is to know God the Father:* "If you really know me, you will know my Father as well." (v 7)
- *To see Jesus is to see God the Father:* "Anyone who has seen me has seen the Father." (v 9)
- *To hear Jesus is to hear God the Father:* "The words I say to you I do not speak on my own authority. Rather, it is the Father, living in me, who is doing his work." (v 10)

This is a man. Yet in this man we encounter God—because this man *is* God. Jesus is the Son of God sent by God to lead us home to God (14 v 2-4). For some people, this is so new and so extraordinary that it's hard to take in. The first disciples were in that category. For others, it's become so familiar that we've lost the wonder. An encounter with Jesus is an encounter with God the Father.

The Spirit, too, doesn't enable us to experience the presence of some other being. He's not a substitute for the real thing. He *is* the real thing. He *is* God and so brings us into contact with the genuine presence of the Father and the Son.

What this means is that we always have communion with God—not a part of God. If I have communion with the Son, then I have communion with the Father and the Spirit. The Spirit is the Spirit of God and the Spirit of Christ. So to be in-dwelt by the Spirit is to be in-dwelt by the Son and the Father.

Let me suggest one reason why this matters. It's all too common for Christians to think of the Son as loving and kind, but to think of the Father as distant and harsh. We may think of the Father as a judge who disapproves of us. Or we may think the Son wins over a reluctant Father so that at least the Father now tolerates us. But this attitude separates the Trinity. What we see in the Son is a revelation of the Father. And this is so not simply because the Son knows the Father. The Son is not like someone saying, "I've spent many hours with him and underneath that harsh exterior he's really very kind and generous". The Father and the Son are one Being with a common will. The attitude of the Son is not simply *like* the attitude of the Father. It *is* the attitude of the Father.

2. THE PRINCIPLE OF UNION AND COMMUNION

John Owen says we have a two-way relationship with God. There is, says Owen, giving and receiving. There is loving and being loved. There is delight and delighting. God gives life, hope, freedom and forgiveness, and we respond by giving God our faith, love and worship.

Salvation is not just about having our sins forgiven and escaping God's judgment. It's not just about being justified so that God regards us as righteous in Christ. It is those things. But it's much, much more. God doesn't simply save us *from* sin and death. He saves us *for* something. Owen speaks of Christ's "great undertaking in his life, death, resurrection, ascension, being a mediator between God and us … *to bring us an enjoyment of God*".[60] Faith in Christ brings us into a real two-way relationship of joy with the triune God.

There are dangers in talking about Christian experience. There's the danger of pursuing experiences for their own sake rather than pursuing God. Experiencing God doesn't always mean emotional highs. Another danger is mistaking emotions generated by other things for a true experience of God. Excellent music and a large congregation will create emotions that may be little different from attending a concert or movie. Building your faith on experiences will prove to be a shaky foundation. Your confidence will tend to fluctuate depending on your mood or circumstances. We're not saved because we experience certain emotions. We're saved through the finished work of Christ—and that's a fact, not a feeling.

But we mustn't so stress the objectivity—the "fact-ness"—of our faith that we lose what Christians used to call the "experiential" nature of faith. We're saved for a genuine relationship with the triune God.

Another danger is having a narrow view of what an experience of God involves. For some people it only really means one thing: direct messages from God. They want to hear God speaking to them—and the more dramatic, the better. Other people reject the idea that God sends special messages. But they can do so in a way that creates the impression that Christianity is a largely intellectual activity in which we merely learn information about God from the Bible. Although these views are polar opposites, they share a common problem: they assume a very narrow view of how we experience God. Throughout this book we've tried to observe the many and varied ways in which God is at work in our lives.

Let's come back to John Owen. He says:

> *Our communion with God consists in his communication of himself to us, with our return to him of that which he requires and accepts, flowing from that union which in Jesus Christ we have with him.*[61]

Owen not only says that we have communion with God. He also says that this communion flows from our union with God through Christ. So our second foundational principle is this: *Our **unity with God** in Christ is the basis of our **community with God** in experience.*

Here's the key point. Our communion with God is two-way, but our union with God is all one-way. It's founded on God's grace.

In much Christian mystical thought, union with God is seen as something we achieve as a result of hours of meditation or self-denial or deep contemplation or religious rituals. The image of a ladder is often used: a ladder we must ascend to connect with God. Union and communion are merged and our union-communion with God is based on our attainments.

People often find this attractive because it offers a spirituality of achievement. They like the idea of becoming "spiritual people" through their own self-effort. It appeals to their pride. But most of us simply find it intimidating. Communion with God sounds unattainable—something for monks and mystics. Ordinary people working in nine-to-five jobs are relegated to second-class Christians.

But the grace of God kicks this ladder of spiritual achievement away. Union with God through Christ is something that God gives us. One of the most common ways the New Testament speaks of Christians is as those who are "in Christ". A Christian is by definition someone who is deeply connected to Christ.

So our union with God is a gift. But actually so is our *communion* with God. That's because it always flows from our union with God. So, just like our union with God, communion with God is not something we achieve. It's something we enjoy as a gift from God. Because it's a two-way relationship, we can neglect that gift. Whether we fully enjoy it depends on our actions. But it's never something we achieve.

Imagine a friend gives you a subscription to a movie channel. You might go for a few weeks without watching a movie and so without enjoying their gift. Then perhaps you remember all those great movies you can access. So you *availing ourselves of a gift*

enjoy watching a couple of movies one week. How much you enjoy those movies is up to you. But you can't claim your enjoyment is the result of your achievement. It would be ridiculous to say, "Because of my hard work and dedication I've enjoyed watching three movies this week". Every movie you watch is a gift from your friend.

So it is with your relationship with the triune God. Every pleasure you have from the relationship is God's gift. While you can neglect the relationship, you can never claim that your enjoyment is the result of your spiritual achievements. Your communion with God is always based on your gracious union with God. Commenting on Exodus 19 v 4-6, Old Testament scholar Alec Motyer says:

> *Status comes by the acts of God; enjoyment by the responsive commitment of obedience. Obedience is not our part in a two-sided bargain, but our grateful response to what the Lord has unilaterally decided and done.*[62]

It's important to recognise this distinction between *union* and *communion*. Our union with God is unilateral or one-sided. And, because it's all God's work, nothing we do can change our *status* with God. But God has saved us so we might have *communion* with him, and this communion with God is two-way. God relates to us and in return we relate to God. So we contribute to the relationship. And therefore what we do can affect our *experience* of God.

Our relationship with God rests on the objective reality of the Father's love, the Son's work and the Spirit's presence. And it's to this that we constantly return. If we're feeling spiritually dry, then we return to our union with Christ. If we're filled with doubt or guilt or fear, then we return to our union with Christ. If we feel nothing, then we return to our union with Christ. If we feel great, but still yearn for more, then we return to our union with Christ. Faith reaches out and lays hold of Christ. Faith lifts its gaze to Christ, seated in heaven. Whatever we feel, we know he's in heaven on our behalf.

Feelings and experience are not the same. I experience my human father's love for me whatever my feelings. He cares for me and I'm the beneficiary of that care—whether today I feel close to him or not. It's the same with my heavenly Father. Growing in faith is learning to discern the Trinity's involvement in our lives even when we don't "feel" that involvement. I may wake up tomorrow morning feeling spiritually dry. I may feel crushed by my guilt or weighed down by my responsibilities. I may feel I lack God's immediate support. But I open my curtains and see that the sun has risen. I recognise by faith that this is God's world. He continues to care for his creation and he continues to care for me. He's fathering me, even if today I feel spiritually dry. I'm experiencing his love even though I don't have any warm sensations inside. "This is the victory that has overcome the world, even our faith" (1 John 5 v 4). Sometimes the victory of faith is a victory over our feelings. The aim of this book has been to equip you for the fight of faith: the fight to recognise the reality of the triune God's involvement in the life of his people.

COMPLETE JOY

The apostle John never got over the realisation that he'd seen the glory of God in the person of Christ. He begins his first letter, "That which was from the beginning, which we have heard, which we have seen with our eyes, which we have looked at and our hands have touched—this we proclaim concerning the Word of life" (1 John 1 v 1). Jesus was not a ghost or a vision. He really had human flesh. But in these verses John doesn't refer to him as "Jesus" or

"Christ". He refers to him as "life". "The life appeared," John says in verse 2. John had heard and seen and touched the One through whom the world was created. Jesus doesn't just give everlasting life; he himself is life—true life. Knowing Jesus means participating in the life of the Trinity. John continues, "We proclaim to you what we have seen and heard, so that you also may have fellowship with us. And our fellowship is with the Father and with his Son, Jesus Christ" (1 John 1 v 3). Then he adds, "We write this to make our joy complete" (1 John 1 v 4).

Jesus appeared so that people might have fellowship or communion with God. Together we participate in the life of the Trinity. We're family with God as our Father, Jesus as our brother, and one another as brothers and sisters. The result is a community in which joy is made complete. The Father delights in his Son, and he delights to share that delight with us. We delight in the Son, and we delight to share that delight with others.

Complete joy!

AFTERWORD:
STANDING IN THE RAIN

It's 5 am in Dublin, Ireland, and I'm standing in the rain waiting for a bus. I'm bored. What should I do? "I should pray," I tell myself. But I don't feel like praying. Praying would be easy if I were cosy and quiet in my study. But I'm standing in the rain. I'd rather the bus just came.

But then I'm writing a book on enjoying God. What would Tim the author say to the Tim in the rain? What does enjoying God look like at this moment? I remember the birdsong I heard as I left the house; that I can still hear. I remember reflecting on the extraordinary capacity for birdsong to lift my spirits, apparently out of all proportion to what it actually is. I see it (as I often do) as a gift from my Father: a sign that his creation was, and is, wonderfully generous (as we saw in chapter 3).

I wouldn't choose to be waiting for a bus at 5 am in the morning. Indeed, I was annoyed when I realised that this was what fulfilling my speaking engagement would involve. I wouldn't choose for it to be raining. In fact, if it were down to me, I'd still be in bed. But clearly this is God's choice and he must have some purpose in it (as we saw in chapter 4). So I make my own choice to enjoy the rain. I actively tune in to its notes and rhythms: the noise it makes as it hits the road blending with the larger drips falling from roofs.

I thank God for the birdsong and commit my journey to him in prayer (as we saw in chapter 5). I'm feeling nervous about my journey (as I always do). Will the bus come? Will I catch my plane? But I rest in God's sovereign care (as we saw in chapter 3).

I run over what's been on my mind. My thoughts have been flitting between a sin I committed two days ago that still weighs on my heart and a situation in which I'm expected to show leadership.

I confess my sin (as we saw in chapter 13). I'd been finding comfort in the Father's mercy. Now I think, too, of Christ in heaven on my behalf and find still more comfort for my wretched heart (as we saw in chapter 6). Then I ask for God's help. I feel my inability to provide leadership. I wonder if people trust me to provide direction. I wonder if I trust myself. But then I remember the Spirit's power. I'm not on my own. God is at work in me and through me by his Spirit (as we saw in chapter 9).

My mind goes back to a verse I read yesterday. *As we contemplate the Lord's glory, we're transformed into his image with ever-increasing glory.* Something like that. I'd reminded my students that we're transformed by gazing on God's glory in Christ. Now I remind myself. Or perhaps the Spirit reminds me (as we saw in chapter 11).

This is a real-life story. I'm not artificially working through the chapters of this book. All of this really happened as described. Perhaps I could have gone on to reflect on Christ's compassion towards me (as we saw in chapter 7). I could have looked back to his reassuring love in bread and wine (as we saw in chapter 8). I could have looked forward with the Spirit's help to a new creation (as we saw in chapter 10). But at this point the bus came.

Here's the point—the main point of this book. At 5 am in the Dublin rain the Father, the Son and the Spirit are all actively engaging with me. And, if I choose, I can respond and enjoy my relationship with them.

The same is true for you right now wherever you are and whatever you're doing.

THANK YOU

Many thanks to my editor, Alison Mitchell, for carefully and cheerfully ensuring that what I've written is coherent and accessible.

ENDNOTES

1 Gregory of Nazianzus, "On Holy Baptism", Oration 40.41; *The Nicene and Post-Nicene Fathers: Second Series* (Hendrickson, 1994), Series 2, Vol. 7, p 375. This version is from the translation of the quote in John Calvin, *The Institutes of Christian Religion*, ed. J. T. McNeill, trans. F. L. Battles (Westminster, 1960), 1.13.17.

2 John Owen, "Communion with God," in *Works*, Vol. 2, ed. William Goold, (Banner of Truth, 1965), p 268.

3 Adapted by the author from Martin Luther, 'The Freedom of a Christian,' (1520), *The Annotated Luther Volume 1: The Roots of Reform*, ed. Timothy J. Wengert (Fortress Press, 2015), p 499-500.

4 Timothy Keller, *King's Cross: The Story of the World in the Life of Jesus* (Hodder & Stoughton, 2011), p 9-10.

5 John Calvin, *The Institutes of Christian Religion*, ed. J. T. McNeill, trans. F. L. Battles, Library of Christian Classics (Philadelphia: Westminster, 1960), 1.17.7.

6 J. I. Packer, *Knowing God* (Hodder & Stoughton, 1973), p 206-207.

7 John Owen, "Communion with God" in *Works*, Vol. 2, p 35.

8 Richard Sibbes, "The Bruised Reed and Smoking Flax" in *Works*, Volume 1 (Banner of Truth, 1973), p 42-43.

9 John Owen, "Communion with God" in *Works*, Vol. 2, p 21, adapted.

10 John Owen, *Communion with God*, abridged by R. J. K. Law (Banner of Truth, 1991), p 13, italics added.

11 See Charles Taylor, *A Secular Age* (Harvard University Press, 2007).

12 Marilynne Robinson, *Housekeeping* (Faber, 1981, 2005), p 11-12.

13 Charles H. Spurgeon, "Prayer, the Cure for Care" in *Metropolitan Tabernacle Sermons No. 2351*, 12 January 1888.

14 John Owen, "Communion with God" in *Works*, Vol. 2, p 22.

15 John Calvin, *Commentary on the Book of Psalms*, trans. James Anderson (Eerdmans, 1948), comments on Psalm 23 v 1, Volume 1, p 390-391, language updated and adapted.

16 Frederick S. Leahy, *The Hand of God: The Comfort of Having a Sovereign God* (Banner of Truth, 2006), p 122.

17 For a more in-depth look at the themes in this chapter see Tim Chester, *God's Discipline: A Word of Encouragement in the Midst of Hardship*, Christian Focus, 2018.

18 See Matthew 5 v 16, 45, 48; 6 v 1, 4, 6 twice, 8, 14, 15, 18 twice, 26, 32; 7 v 11.

19 John Calvin, *The Institutes of Christian Religion*, ed. J. T. McNeill, trans. F. L. Battles (Westminster, 1960), 3.20.36.

20 I have changed their names to protect their anonymity.

21 C. H. Spurgeon, "The Relationship of Marriage" in *The Metropolitan Tabernacle Pulpit*, Vol. 13 (1867), (Pilgrim Publications, 1974), Sermon no. 762.

22 See William Lane, *Hebrews 9-13*, Word Biblical Commentary (Word, TX, 1991), p 410-411; and Paul Ellingworth, *The Epistle to the Hebrews*, The New International Greek Testament Commentary (Paternoster, MI, 1993), p 639-640.

23 This section draws upon the work of Matthew Sleeman, *Geography and the Ascension Narrative in Acts* (Cambridge University Press, 2009); and Matthew Sleeman, "The Ascension and Heavenly Ministry of Christ" in *The Forgotten Christ*, ed. Stephen Clark (IVP UK, 2007) p 140-189.

24 John Owen, "Communion with God" in *Works*, Vol. 2, p 194.

25 John Owen, "Communion with God" in *Works*, Vol. 2, p 194, modernised.

26 John Owen, "Communion with God" in *Works*, Vol. 2, p 194.

27 From Horatio G. Spafford, "When peace like a river attendeth my way" (1873).

28 John Owen, "Communion with God" in *Works*, Vol. 2, p 194-195.

29 John Owen, "'Communion with God" in *Works*, Vol. 2, p 195, modernised.

30 See John Owen, "Sacramental Discourses: Discourse XXII" in *Works*, Vol. 9, ed. William Goold (Banner of Truth, 1965), p 612-614.

31 Thomas Goodwin, "The Heart of Christ in Heaven Towards Sinners on Earth", *Works*, Vol. 4 (James Nichol, 1862), p 112.

32 Adapted from Thomas Goodwin, "The Heart of Christ", p 116.

33 Thomas Goodwin, "The Heart of Christ", as above, p 136.

34 Thomas Goodwin, "The Heart of Christ", as above, p 121-122, modernised.

35 Thomas Goodwin, "The Heart of Christ", as above, p 146.

36 Thomas Goodwin, "The Heart of Christ", as above, p 149, modernised.

37 Thomas Goodwin, "The Heart of Christ", as above, p 149-150, modernised.

38 Thomas Goodwin, "The Heart of Christ", as above, p 115, modernised.

39 Adapted from William Bridge, *A Lifting Up for the Downcast* (Banner of Truth, 1961), p 62-66.

40 Francis Chan, *The Forgotten God: Reversing Our Tragic Neglect of the Holy Spirit* (David C. Cook, 2009), p 143, 150, 156.

41 For more on the way the gospel brings change to our lives, see my book *You Can Change: God's Transforming Power For Our Sinful Behaviour and Negative Emotions* (IVP/Crossway, 2008/2010).

42 Russell Moore, "Adoption and the Renewal of Creation", Together For Adoption Conference 2009. I have also used this story in Tim Chester and Christopher De la Hoyde, *Who on Earth is the Holy Spirit?* (The Good Book Company, 2013), p 50.

43 John Calvin, *The Institutes of Christian Religion*, ed. J. T. McNeill, trans. F. L. Battles (Westminster, 1960), 3.9.

44 John Calvin, *Calvin's Commentaries: The Epistles of Paul the Apostle to the Romans and the Thessalonians*, trans. Ross Mackenzie, eds. D.W. & T.F. Torrance (St Andrew's Press, 1961), p 105, commentary on Romans 5 v 2.

45 This chapter is adapted from Tim Chester, *Bible Matters: Meeting God in His Word* (IVP, 2017).

46 Tim Chester, *Bible Matters: Meeting God in his Word* (IVP, 2017), p 35.

47 John Calvin, *Sermons on the Epistle to the Ephesians*, Sermon on Ephesians 4 v 11-12 (Banner of Truth, 1973), p 368.

48 Wayne Grudem, *1 Peter*, Tyndale New Testament Commentaries (IVP, 1988), p 97.

49 Dietrich Bonhoeffer, *Life Together and Psalms: Prayerbook of the Bible* (Fortress, 2005), p 32.

50 Dietrich Bonhoeffer, *Life Together and Psalms: Prayerbook of the Bible* (Fortress, 2005), p 31-32.

51 For more on the role of meals in building community, see my book *A Meal with Jesus: Discovering Grace, Community, and Mission around the Table* (Crossway/IVP, 2011/2011).

52 A. W. Tozer, *The Knowledge of the Holy* (BiblioTech Press, 2016), p 1.

53 John Calvin, *The Institutes of Christian Religion*, trans. F.L. Battles, ed. J.T. McNeill (Westminster Press/SCM, 1961), 1.5.3.

54 John Owen, "Communion with God," *Works*, Vol. 2, ed. William Goold (Banner of Truth, 1965). *Communion with God* is available with modern spellings, headings and formatting under the title *Communion with the Triune God*, eds. Kelly M. Kapic and Justin Taylor (Crossway, 2007). The easiest version to read is the abridged modernised version by John Owen, *Communion with God*, ed. R. J. K. Law (Banner of Truth, 1991).

55 John Owen, "Communion with God", *Works*, Vol. 2, 9.

56 John Calvin, *The Institutes of Christian Religion*, ed. J. T. McNeill, trans. F. L. Battles (Westminster, 1960), 1.13.1.

57 John Calvin, *The Institutes of Christian Religion*, ed. J. T. McNeill, trans. F. L. Battles (Westminster, 1960), 1.13.2.

58 John Owen, "Communion with God", *Works*, Vol. 2, p 15, modernised.

59 John Owen, *Works*, "Communion with God", Vol. 2, p 15, modernised.

60 John Owen, "Communion with God", *Works*, Vol. 2, p 78, emphasis added.

61 John Owen, "Communion with God", *Works*, Vol. 2, p 8-9, modernised.

62 Alec Motyer, *The Message of Exodus*, The Bible Speaks Today, (IVP, 2005), p 200.

PRACTICAL GUIDES TO BOOST YOUR PRAYER LIFE

Transform your prayer life with fresh prayer ideas drawn straight from Scripture. Because when we pray in line with God's priorities as found in his word, our prayers are powerful and effective (James 5 v 16)—and that's a truly thrilling prospect.

thegoodbook.com/5things
thegoodbook.co.uk/5things

EXPOSITORY GUIDES
BY TIM CHESTER

This series of expository guides walks you through books of the Bible verse by verse. Read them simply as a book; use them to feed on God's word as a daily devotional, complete with reflection questions; or use them as you prepare to lead small-group Bible studies or teach in your church.

thegoodbook.com/foryou
thegoodbook.co.uk/foryou

thegoodbook
COMPANY

BIBLICAL | RELEVANT | ACCESSIBLE

At The Good Book Company, we are dedicated to helping Christians and local churches grow. We believe that God's growth process always starts with hearing clearly what he has said to us through his timeless word—the Bible.

Ever since we opened our doors in 1991, we have been striving to produce Bible-based resources that bring glory to God. We have grown to become an international provider of user-friendly resources to the Christian community, with believers of all backgrounds and denominations using our books, Bible studies, devotionals, evangelistic resources, and DVD-based courses.

We want to equip ordinary Christians to live for Christ day by day, and churches to grow in their knowledge of God, their love for one another, and the effectiveness of their outreach.

Call us for a discussion of your needs or visit one of our local websites for more information on the resources and services we provide.

Your friends at The Good Book Company

NORTH AMERICA   thegoodbook.com   866 244 2165
UK & EUROPE   thegoodbook.co.uk   0333 123 0880
AUSTRALIA   thegoodbook.com.au   (02) 9564 3555
NEW ZEALAND   thegoodbook.co.nz   (+64) 3 343 2463

WWW.CHRISTIANITYEXPLORED.ORG
Our partner site is a great place for those exploring the Christian faith, with a clear explanation of the good news, powerful testimonies and answers to difficult questions.